Cover design and photo by Emily Lowrie

Golf Above the Shoulders
Little Things to Enhance the Enjoyment of Your Game

To my four blessings

Crista
Bobby
Emily

Olivia

Copyright 2017 All Rights Reserved

Golf Above the Shoulders – Little things to enhance your game

Table of Contents

Introduction – What are we talking about? 6

Golf: Still a Pure Sport 11

The Game's Greatest Thinkers 14

    Not a Solo Act 22

HOW TO PRACTICE 24

    It starts on the Practice Tee 24

    How to Make Changes to Your Swing 29

    Don't Practice with Plastic Golf Balls 31

    How to Hit Balls from a Grass Area 33

    Get Yourself a Full-Length Mirror 37

    Invest in Golf Lessons 40

    Don't Hit Irons from Plastic Mats 44

    Tempo Drills 48

EQUIPMENT 50

    How to Select the Right Clubs 50

    The Truth about Shafts 56

    The Proper Size Grip 65

    How to Put Grips on a Club 67

    The Confidence of Clean Clubs 75

    What Ball Is Best for Your Game? 78

THE SWING 86

    Let's Get a Little Technical 86

Golf Above the Shoulders – Little things to enhance your game

- A Word about the Swing Plane 90
- The Swing Thought 96
- Lining up at Address 100
- Lining Up the Clubface 102
- The Fast Track to Contact 106
- The Transition 111
- The Hitting Zone 113
- The Waggle 115
- The Pre-Shot Routine 117
- Know Your Game, Trust Your Swing 121
- Putting It All Together 125

COURSE MANAGEMENT AND STRATEGY 127

- Plan a Strategy for each Hole 127
- Selecting Your Target 130
- Analyze the Wind Velocity 133
- Hitting to Different Elevations 137

GOLF COURSE ETIQUITTE 141

- Replace Divots 142
- Repair Ball Marks 144
- Keep Cool 155
- How to remove the ball from the cup 158
- Rake the trap when you are done 159
- Broken tees 160

Golf Above the Shoulders – Little things to enhance your game

Proper Dress 163
Don't take a practice divot 166
Kill Bugs, Not Grass 167
Hitting Sequence Around the Green 168
Line Up Your Putt in a Reasonable Time 169
Keep the Pace of Play 170
Marking the Score Card 172
Where to Stop Your Cart While on the Green ... 173
Lost Balls 174
Follow Local Cart Rules 175
Snowman Max 177
Play Ready Golf on Weekends 178
Drinking on the course 179
Know the official rules 180

EXTRA STUFF 182

Pin Position Indicators 182
How to Watch Golf 185
Join the USGA 192
Register for a Handicap 194
How to use the Handicap 196
PGA Tour Phone APP 197
Little Side Games to Add to the Fun 198
The Calloway Handicap System 200

Golf Above the Shoulders – Little things to enhance your game

> The Scramble Format 204
>
> The Better Ball of Partners 206
>
> Alternate Shot 207
>
> Epilogue 207

Golf Above the Shoulders
Important things you don't hear about

Introduction – What are we talking about?

My 10-year old daughter and my father-in-law were my inspiration for writing this book. She had been playing golf for two years and progressing faster than her friends that we play with that have been playing longer. When she was five years old, she started hitting golf balls in our backyard. By the end of the summer, she was hitting them over the roof and onto the front yard of the house across the street! That ended our back yard as a practice area.

One day at the driving range, my father in law was watching my daughter hit balls and he was listening to my instructions to her. He noted that the things I was telling her were not the standard type of things you get from a typical golf lesson. I had not really paid much attention to the fact that I was teaching her concepts that were not the usual mechanics of the swing. There were mechanics, of course, but only about 50% of what I was teaching her pertained to swing mechanics. The other

50% dealt with the mental side of the game; the thinking part. My father in law said I had a knack for teaching golf and that I should share it with all golfers. I just laughed it off at the time.

When I was younger, I was a golf instructor and I taught the conventional set of swing mechanics that all golf instructors teach. It was only after I left the golf profession to pursue a career in science that I realized I had missed some very important aspects of the game- and in fact, no other pros that I knew were teaching these concepts either. The ideas missing in a standard golf lesson involve what should be going on above the shoulders. In other words, no one was teaching their students how to think about the game- only how to execute the mechanics.

As a result many people that take one or more golf lessons, usually do not get as much benefit out of the lesson as they potentially could. The main reason is that they were not taught how or what to think about in a practice session or on the golf course.

There are countless books and instructional videos about the power of positive thinking, how to get the most out of a practice session, building confidence and dealing with the frustration this great game brings to all of us. Millions of words have been written about the proper mental approach to the game and how to take strokes off of your score. Most are good and valid in their concept, and I recommend that everyone should read these materials on the positive self-awareness of the game.

However, that is not what this book is about. There are some actual things you can put into action to implement these philosophical concepts that the experts don't write about. In this little book, my intention is to arm you with some actual implementation tools that will improve the mental side of your game and make each round a fun and rewarding experience.

While working as a golf pro, and in the subsequent years to follow, I have gained much insight into how the experts play the game and what is lacking in the games of the 80's and 90's (and above) players. I have spent much time experimenting with equipment and concepts, and have observed details of the way the Touring Pros play their games.

If you try to incorporate some or all of these ideas as part of your golf experience, you will gain confidence, be more fulfilled each time you play and maybe even cut a few strokes off your score.

The confidence will come knowing that you are prepared for each shot and the fulfillment will grow within you as you become more personally involved with your game. Instead of your round of golf just happening, you will be making it happen by being in control of your shots leaving much less to chance. You can get so much more out of your experiences on the course than just a score and a beer after the round. After all, you have just invested five hours of your day and a few dollars. You should come away with relaxed fulfillment regardless of your score.

I hope you enjoy what I have to say in this book, and learn a few new things that you

Golf Above the Shoulders – Little things to enhance your game

> can take to the course the next time you play.

The natural beauty of a golf course on a perfect summer day is a glimpse of what heaven must be like!

Golf: Still a Pure Sport

What do I mean by a "Pure Sport"? Golf is a game where true competition is still the foundation of the game. It is not subject to the liberal ideas of non-competition-everybody-is-the-same nonsense at all levels and ages.

Among professional ranks, there is no minor league, no second string, nor bench sitters collecting salaries. On the Tour, if you don't make the cut, you don't win any money. This keeps the caliber of play at the highest level.

After a tournament season, if a player has not played well enough to earn a certain amount of money, he loses his card, meaning he loses his privileges to continue to play on the Tour. That player will have to go back through the qualifying tournament again to regain his/her Tour card.

There are no players on the "bench" collecting a salary until they are good enough to make a cut as a Monday Qualifier. There are minor professional tours, but the scenario is still the same; no money for no game.

Character and integrity are paramount to the game. It is the only sport where the player calls a penalty on himself if they have violated a rule. In an official tournament, if a ball moves when the player is removing debris from around it, the player is required to notify an official of the violation and incur a penalty. That is a powerful statement about the level of integrity of the people playing the game.

To my knowledge, there are no felons playing the Tour, no players are covered in tattoos nor involved in questionable behavior. When someone does become involved in behavior below the standards of conduct for the Tour, they are penalized either officially, or unofficially. Professional golf is still about character and integrity and that is what makes the game great!

Golf Above the Shoulders – Little things to enhance your game

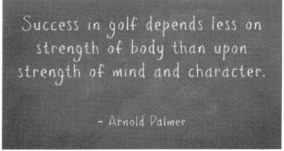

Arnold Palmer is the personification of character and integrity; the cornerstones of this great game. Through the years, I have met Mr. Palmer several times. Once I sent him a large box full of items for him to sign for a silent auction at a Red Cross Tournament I was organizing. Included was a check for the return postage. He sent everything back signed in just a few days, including my check for the postage. He paid the postage himself. His signed items were a big hit at the silent auction!

Golf Above the Shoulders – Little things to enhance your game

The Game's Greatest Thinkers

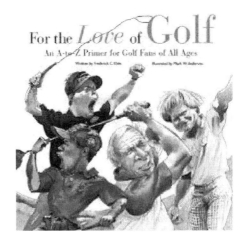

The professional golf circuits are an assemblage of the best strategists and thinkers in the game. A player cannot attain that level of expertise without the highest levels of swing mechanics and mental stability. Any tour player is capable of winning on any given week, yet only a limited number of players actually win tournaments. Assuming most have sound swing mechanics, there are two other factors that determine whether a player can win or not. First they must have the mental stability that allows their swing to hold up under pressure, and second, they must have the proper playing strategy that will maximize their personal ability with the challenges of the golf course. In order to accomplish this, the player must know his game, and know the details of the course. The former requires practice, concentration and confidence while the latter is usually the responsibility of the player's partner- his caddie. The caliber of play is so high that there is very little luck involved in winning. It is the ability to function under pressure combined with a sound playing strategy that will win a golf tournament.

One of the greatest challenges for golfers at any level of ability, including the Pros, is how to effectively take what they have practiced and learned at the practice tee to the first tee on the golf course. There are several ways to do this, and we will discuss them as we move along.

Of course, you don't become a **good** player without thinking about what you are doing out on the golf course. Conversely, you don't become a **great** player without great thinking either. For an average player, the round just happens. For a good player, there is some strategy and awareness of the course conditions. For the great player, what goes on above the shoulders becomes paramount to a low score. In my opinion, here are a few of the game's greatest thinkers (in no particular order). The list is surely not complete and I am doing an injustice to many of the great players by not listing them here because, as mentioned above, you can't make it to the tour without a good mental approach and process. All of the tour players are focused thinkers, with the ability to win on any particular week, however some players have stood out in history as great thinkers and their accomplishments speak for their mental abilities as well as their physical talent.

Golf Above the Shoulders – Little things to enhance your game

As a young pro, I attended as many tournaments as I could, looking for clues to the game. I looked for the kinds of things that no one teaches in a golf lesson. Details of the game that I could bring back to my own students, or use myself.

Each time I watched Jack Nicklaus I was amazed at his approach to each shot. He was as intense a player as I have ever seen. The way he analyzed the weather conditions, and the course conditions, he made each shot he hit an entire sporting event in itself. I got the feeling that nothing was ever wasted. Every shot he hit was well thought out, planned and perfectly executed. No wasted shots nor bad risks taken. This was exemplified in the 1984 Masters when Jack, at the age of 46, became the oldest player to win the Masters. That afternoon in April was one of the most exciting sporting events in history. Nicklaus studied and planned each shot, then executed perfectly with focus and concentration. That day he won his 18th major. You can see highlights of the last day on YouTube. It is worth taking a few minutes to watch- you will be inspired.

Ben Hogan, one of the greatest shotmakers in the history of the game, believed that any golfer with average coordination can learn to break eighty—if one applies oneself patiently and intelligently. With the techniques revealed in his classic book, you can learn how to make your game work from tee to green, step-by-step and stroke by stroke.

Even though he is shorter off the tee (averaging 252 yards per drive) than virtually every top player in the game, Corey Pavin turned that weakness into his strength. Because he cannot overpower a golf course, Pavin became one of the game's great thinkers and manipulators of the ball. Never was this more evident than at Shinnecock Hills Golf Club on Sunday, June 18, 1995, the last day of the US Open which he won. He said, "I never put the ball in a position where I could not make par." There is a lot behind this concise statement. It implies a pre- game plan, astute knowledge of the course, a good caddie, great focus and concentration, and of course, great and consistent execution.

In addition to learning how to practice, you will also learn how to think like Moe Norman, one of the greatest thinkers on and off the golf course. In doing so, you will master how to take your game from the practice tee to the golf course; what Moe called the "longest walk in golf".

In an interview I once saw with Greg Norman (no relation), he also said that he struggled with taking the "practice tee to the first tee"

You can imagine that if it is difficult for these great players to execute on the golf course what they have learned in their practice sessions, than it is really challenging for an average golfer to do so.

Golf Above the Shoulders – Little things to enhance your game

The greatest international player of all time is Gary Player. Mr. Player was a great strategist and shot maker and probably the best sand player the game has ever seen. Although at 5'7" he is most noted for his dedication to physical fitness, his mental fitness and intelligence has won him many tournaments.

Then there is the great Tiger Woods. The only man in the modern era of golf to win four consecutive majors- the grand slam. Tiger won the Masters, the US Open, the British Open and the PGA in succession, completing the Grand Slam of golf. The only controversy concerning this accomplishment is that it spanned two golf seasons. I see this as a minor detail. Winning these four events in succession is what counts and no one else has done it. He maintained golf perfection for a long time to accomplish this which required mental and physical perfection.

At the time of this writing, the current #1 player is Jordon Speith. He is a great player with sound mechanics, a great attitude, and accomplished strategist at a young age. Jordon has not yet reached his full potential. It will be exciting to watch his career evolve.

As you read on, you will pick up some details of the game that you can incorporate into each round you play. As you develop your swing thought and pre-shot routine (covered later in detail), you will be better equipped to take your "practice session to the first tee". This means that you will have to take these mental issues as seriously as your swing mechanics and practice these mental concepts during your practice sessions along with your physical swing mechanics.

Be patient. Building sound mental and physical habits take time but they will develop if you stay with therm. As you refine your swing thought and pre-shot routine on the practice tee, then it will be automatic when you go out to play. You will be able to overcome the "first tee jitters".

Golf Above the Shoulders – Little things to enhance your game

Not a Solo Act

Even though golf appears to be a test of one player against the golf course, it really is a team effort for the great players. On the course, the player-caddie combination is the basic team. The caddie is a critical part of the success of the golfer hitting the shots. The caddie's knowledge of the course combined with their understanding of how their player executes with each club, makes the caddie an indispensable part of the team.

Off the course, the players have one or more coaches. At least one coach for the swing mechanics, and often times another mental coach for help on maintaining mental stability dealing with the pressure of playing at the highest levels.

Great players are also supported by their families and sometimes financial backers early in their career.

Average amateur golfers do not have the benefit of all of these support personnel. Most players have never used a caddie and do not have a mental coach. They usually have a limited time to play a round of golf and are planning their finish time before they hit their first shot. By playing intelligently, a player can optimize the limited time they have to play, and maximize their enjoyment.

Each time you play a golf course, keep your eyes open to the characteristics of the course. Make mental notes on the positions of sand traps, grassy moguls, water hazards, etc., even if you do not land in these hazards. Your mental log of these things may help you the next time you play that course. The more often you play a course, the more "local knowledge" you will gain, and the better your playing strategy will become.

The pros keep little note books with them as they play to remind them of course details that they noted during their practice rounds. When you watch a tournament on TV, you will always see them looking at their notes.

You don't have to carry a notebook with you when you play, just be aware of the course conditions as you play even if they do not affect your game that particular day.

HOW TO PRACTICE

It starts on the Practice Tee

Many books and videos have been produced regarding how to practice and how to get the most out of your practice sessions. I will not go into that here except to say that practice makes perfect- or imperfect. You want to be careful to practice the correct things for your abilities, age, body type and gender. This is the main reason I advocate and recommend that everyone takes a few lessons or a full series from a PGA professional. PGA Pros are well trained and the standards are high to get into the PGA. They have to be able to play as well as teach. Add to those mechanics, the ideas you will pick up from this book, and you will have a better start than 90% of the people that step up to the first tee.

Now you may hate to practice, or not have the time to practice or maybe you don't even hit a few balls before you tee off (you really should warm up a little before you play). You will still benefit from the ideas here, it will just take a little longer to make these ideas part of your game. The little details I am suggesting require just as much practice to implement into your game as the mechanics of the swing.

Practice comes in two forms, a full out practice session at the driving range, and the pre-round warm-up session where you hit 15 or 20 shots before you tee off.

In the practice session, you are working on some mechanics and most of the ideas in this book. In the warm-up session before you play, you are moving your muscles and also checking to see how you are hitting the ball that day. One of the frustrations of this great game is that the human body does not always do the same things from day to day. There are many reasons why our swing may vary from round to round, but the fact of the matter is that it just does vary and you have to be in tune with how you are hitting the ball on any particular day.

For the Pro's, the variation is a lot less from day to day than it is for the rest of us. Nevertheless, you use the warm-up time to assess how you are moving and hitting the ball that day. Variations are fine and you need to understand what they are before you play.

Let's say you usually hit a pretty straight shot but on one particular day, your shots are all fading a little. Maybe you slept a little crooked or have a stiff muscle in your side, etc. It doesn't matter what is causing the fade, but the fact is, you are hitting fades this day. When you go to play your round, wisdom and logic say to play for the fade when you pick your targets. It makes no sense to line up like always, or like you think you should be aligned when you know you will not hit the spot. Use the feedback you gained from the warm-up shots and make the minor adjustment on the course. It can make the difference of being in the fairway or in the trees. Always pay attention to your shots as you play your round too, and make minor adjustments to your line-up (only- don't try to make mechanical swing changes during a round).

Finally, use your warm up time to settle into your swing thought and pre-shot routine. These two items will be discussed in detail later. Always have your swing thought in mind before your hit any shot, either on the practice tee, or on the course. The shots you warm up with before you play, are good opportunities to settle into your swing thought and get the most out of your warm-up.

Basically, the first few shots you hit to start your day are not going to be good. The muscles of your body need to get moving in sync with each other and that takes several shots to establish. You can do this on the practice tee, or on the course. Since it could take about 10 shots to get everything moving properly (especially as you get older), you can leave these bad shots in the driving range field, or you can expend them over the first few holes of your round and get yourself off to a bad start!

How to Make Changes to Your Swing

You can hit balls for an hour or more and come away from your practice session with nothing to take to the golf course. During a practice session at the driving range, most golfers shooting in the high 80's and 90's (and above), just hit random shots, one after another. They have no specific target and try to make different swing adjustments with each shot.

Effective swing changes take time and practice to perfect. Don't try to analyze each and every shot. Rather, keep executing the thing you are working on and look for trends in the results. The results of changes you make to your swing are statistical and will not give you the desired result after one or two swings. You have to see a pattern in your results moving toward your desired improvement/change over time. True, lasting improvements take time and practice to ingrain in your mind and muscles.

You should pick out one thing to work on and stay with it until it begins to happen on a consistent basis. This implies, of course, that you are working on the correct things. That is where one or more golf lessons would be helpful in guiding you down the proper path to a successful swing.

You just have to be realistic. Do not expect to fix something in a few minutes, or during a round of golf. That kind of scenario is counter-productive for sure. Too many golfers will instantly analyze their swing problems after each shot on the course while playing a round of golf. You will hear, "I lifted my head", and then on the next shot, "… swung too fast", and then the next shot, "…didn't shift my weight" etc. You cannot play golf this way, nor have any fun playing.

You have to stay with the swing you have while on the course, and make incremental changes at the practice tee.

Don't Practice with Plastic Golf Balls

Plastic golf balls are cheap and seem like a good idea to hit around in your back yard but there are a few major problems with using them to practice. They are basically useless as practice tools.

The first major problem is that you get absolutely no feel of the ball and the club. If you try to use them for chipping, you will gain absolutely nothing and may actually hurt your ability to chip from off the green. You need to swing harder with plastic balls and you will not build up any sense of feel for distance. Chipping from, say, from 50 yards in, is strictly about feel. You need to use real balls to develop this feel.

Second, they do not give an accurate flight, so you cannot use them to see your shot's trajectory. They are prone to hook and slice especially if there is a little breeze.

Finally, they sit up in the grass which encourages you to hit up at the ball- a fatal flaw in any golf swing.

Golf Above the Shoulders – Little things to enhance your game

A good alternative is to get yourself a full-length mirror for the garage and practice swing positions in front of it. Get a good book or magazine with sequential photos (of a player with a similar body type as yours), and emulate the positions in the stop action photos. Get the feel of your body positions for each photo frame. You will gain much more from this exercise.

How to Hit Balls from a Grass Area

There is a proper and professional way to hit golf balls from a grass practice area. The grass found on a golf course is very expensive and if you are the member of a private or semi-private club, there is most likely the same grass on the practice tee area as there is on the fairways. As a member, or a public player, you really have a responsibility to minimize the amount of turf you tear up during a practice session. It takes a few of months for the new seed to grow in and be plush enough to get to fairway quality. If you want the advantage of practicing off of a quality practice tee, then please minimize your divots. If many golfers hit off the grass to practice, it will not take much time for the practice tees to be completely torn up and unusable. At that point you lose the advantage of hitting from fairway-like conditions.

The proper way to hit from a grass practice area is to place each ball just behind the divot of the previous shot so that 90% of the new divot will be going into the area of the first divot. The result at the end of your practice session will be a circular-type spot

Golf Above the Shoulders – Little things to enhance your game

where all of the turf is gone, and the total area of divots is at a minimum. See the pictures below.

It is much more efficient to repair a larger area of missing grass, than to try to fill in individual divots that were made from each shot. Not only does the practice area become unusable quickly, it also can get lumpy and require a lot of maintenance time to keep it in quality condition.

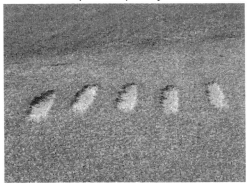

Golf Above the Shoulders – Little things to enhance your game

The wrong way to use a practice tee is shown here. Random shots with no regard to the turf will result in a progressively deteriorating practice area. The picture below shows the extreme case of abuse and an unusable practice area.

A practice area like the one shown below is ugly, costly to fix, and generally undesirable to use for iron play.

Golf Above the Shoulders – Little things to enhance your game

After you hit the first shot and make the first divot, the next shot should come from the location of the ball in this picture. When the next shot is hit, most of the new divot will occur in the area of the first divot. Just the ball should be on the grass area, which is all you need to hit a golf shot.

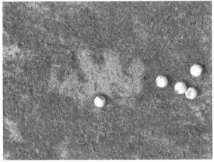

Although this is maybe still spread out a little bit, the player here has tried to consolidate his shots into the one area. This is much better for a practice session than the pictures shown above. It is easier to repair a larger area, than to try to fix individual divots.

Get Yourself a Full-Length Mirror

When you go out to play, you should wear nice clothes to build your confidence but that is not the reason for the mirror!

Put a cheap full-length mirror in the garage or basement that you can use to see parts of you swing. You can view your swing in stop-action as you hold a pose from the front or the side. By doing this, you get the feel of what the proper positions should feel like during your swing.

There are many books and magazines, not to mention the internet, available with stop-action sequential photos of all of the great golfers. Find someone with a physical build like yours and emulate the sequences of the frames in front of the mirror. You will be surprised at what you learn about your swing and how your muscles feel by using a mirror and a set of photos.

Some golf instructors use mirrors with their lessons.

Just be a little careful when swinging in the house or basement. In my lifetime I have destroyed at least three lamps and a kitchen hanging fixture!

Golf Above the Shoulders – Little things to enhance your game

Oops!

Golf Above the Shoulders – Little things to enhance your game

Invest in Golf Lessons

Each time you play a round of golf you are spending (or investing) anywhere from $40 up to $75. Golf can be an expensive sport yet many people will not invest $100 in a golf lesson.

When you purchase a new item, say an electronic item, you read the user's manual in order to get the most out of your device. Why not get the most out of your golf investment by learning how to play the game properly in order to get the greatest payback in terms of personal satisfaction and enjoyment.

A good PGA Professional will show you how to get the most from your physical characteristics. The longer you wait to get a few lessons, the harder it will be to break those old habits. If you are waiting for the day that you walk out onto the first tee and, like a miracle, start hitting the ball long and straight down the middle you may be waiting for a time longer than the years you have left to play. You are looking for a phantom alternative to your current swing.

What you need to make that alternative really happen is knowledge of the proper swing mechanics for your body. That is just what a trained Professional can give you. No two bodies are the same and hence, no two swings are exactly the same.

Another benefit you will derive from your Pro, is how to select the proper equipment that will optimize your results. I will have more to say about that in a later topic. So, resist the urge to spend $300 for the latest driver that looks like an anvil at the end of the shaft, and instead, invest part of that into a few golf lessons and get the most out of your current equipment until advised to upgrade.

Golf Above the Shoulders – Little things to enhance your game

Realistically, there is no magic stick that will automatically allow you to start hitting the ball like the tour players. It is interesting to note how the PGA Tour scoring averages have not changed too much over the time the records have been kept. 1947 was the first year the PGA awarded the Vardon Trophy to the player with the lowest scoring average who played at least 60 rounds in the year.

In 1947, the award went to Jimmy Demaret with a scoring average of 69.90. In 2013, the award went to Tiger Woods with an average of 68.99. That's a difference of .91 strokes over at least 60 rounds of golf; less than one stroke! Now when you are shooting in the high 60's one stroke is significant when averaged out for the season. But with all of the technological advancements in golf balls, clubhead design and alloys, and the same things with shafts, .91 strokes does not seem like very much improvement. What this says, is that the players of the late 1940's, at least Jimmy Demaret anyway, was a pretty good striker of the ball! Using his old equipment he would have been able to win money on today's modern Tour.

So, what I am trying to illustrate here is that the equipment is only a second-order improvement to your game. Solid swing fundamentals are the basis for achieving good scores. So, the next time you have the urge to buy that new driver, instead sign up for a few lessons first. When you have made the improvements to your swing from your lessons, then go buy that driver. It will seem to work better for you AFTER the lessons.

Golf Above the Shoulders – Little things to enhance your game

Don't Hit Irons from Plastic Mats

Driving ranges typically have a tee line of square plastic mats with a foam backing made to resemble turf. It is a low maintenance solution for the driving range rather than trying to maintain a grass practice area. If hitting off of these mats is your only option, then by all means use them rather than skip a practice session.

If, however, you have the option of going to a grassy area to hit balls, you should always choose the grass over the artificial turf to get a more accurate assessment of how you are hitting the ball.

Particularly with the irons, when you hit off of the plastic grass, your club will slide into the ball if you hit it fat and you will get a resulting shot that is not indicative of how you actually hit the ball. On real grass, if you hit fat, your shot is usually dead. You rip up a big divot and the ball just plops out a few yards. When you hit behind the ball on a plastic mat, your club will bounce a little and slide into the ball producing a shot that does not look too bad giving a false sense of success. If you keep practicing that way, you will be doing more harm than good to your swing because you will never get an accurate idea of how you are actually hitting.

Byron Nelson once said that a proper divot should be about the size of a dollar bill in front of the ball without going too deep. A plastic mat eliminates the divot and hence, your understanding of how well or how bad your shot really was.

Golf Above the Shoulders – Little things to enhance your game

The proper position of a divot occurs in front of the ball. The circle above, indicates where the ball was before the shot. The divot should not be any bigger than a dollar bill.

Always pay attention to your divot. It tells you a lot about how your club came through the hitting zone. If you came too steep into the ball, the divot will be deep and maybe start behind the ball rather than in front of the ball. You may also see that the direction of the divot indicated that you cut across the ball from the outside in, indicating a poor weight shift, or a turn that kept you outside, etc. Your divot can give you a lot of information about each shot both on the practice tee and on the golf course.

As a young pro, I used to hit about 600 to 700 balls every day. I loved to hit balls (and still do) as much as playing. I spent many hours hitting off of plastic mats because it was convenient. It took a few months to realize that this was slowing down the progress of improving my swing.

Another annoyance of hitting off of plastic mats is the buildup of the green plastic coating on the bottom of your clubs. Maybe if bothers you, maybe not, but the fact of the matter is, that it builds up a coating on the bottom of your expensive clubs, especially the irons. I don't really know if it has an effect on your game (probably not), but if you spent $1,000 for a nice set of clubs, why would you want to junk them up?

Golf Above the Shoulders – Little things to enhance your game

Tempo Drills

The most common problems I see among amateur golfers relate to tempo and rhythm (myself included).

Many players swing too fast which prevents all of the muscle groups to work together with the proper timing. Muscle strength does not translate into kinetic energy of the clubhead. Clubhead speed is what builds a powerful swing. Maximum clubhead speed comes from the muscle groups of the body working together in rhythm. The transfer of that kinetic energy from the clubhead to the ball is what moves the ball. Everyone has their maximum speed that they can generate. Everyone has their own rhythm which you have to find through practice.

An effective way to find the natural maximum speed your body can generate is by using a tempo drill. It's very simple. On the practice tee, you make shots with a short iron at ¼ speed. Make a full, deliberate swing and make contact with the ball. Make at least five of these shots. Then make 5 fore shots at ½ speed, being sure to make full contact. Resist the urge to speed up, especially if you make a few good shots at half speed.

Next, go to ¾ speed with at least five more shots. You may be surprised to see that you are making pretty good contact with the ball.

Finally, go to full power for at least five more shots and you may see some deterioration in the results from the ¾ shots. It turns out that you will probably make your best shots at 80% body power. The reason is that at 80% body power, your muscle groups have time to coordinate with each other leading to maximum speed generation. I am using the term "body power" here to indicate your feeling of trying to forcibly "create" a swing. If you allow your body to function at its' optimum rhythm, the swing will actually create itself (assuming proper fundamentals). This tempo drill applies to all skill levels.

EQUIPMENT

How to Select the Right Clubs

We just discussed how equipment is not as important as the swing fundamentals. Once you have mastered some of the basics, you will want to get a nice set of clubs that have eye appeal to you at address, and give you confidence over the ball. There are a few things to look for when you are making a decision on a new set of clubs.

The first thing, and most important thing is the **"lie"** of the club. The lie of the club is more important than the length or flex of the shaft. The lie of the club is the angle the club head makes with the shaft. When you are address, the sole of the club should be even on the ground. The toe should not be up in the air, nor should the heal of the club head be up in the air. The sole should be flat on the ground. When the toe is in the air, the club will have a tendency to pull or hook the ball and vice versa if the heal is off the ground. Secondly, when the lie is wrong for your swing, your shots will result in having a little side spin instead of backspin producing sometimes unexpected bounces or trajectories. Even if you are playing a course with many side-hill lies, the proper lie of your irons is still important because the side-hill lies of the fairways will exacerbate or magnify the improper lie on your clubs. Your PGA Professional can help you with this, or you can figure it out for yourself as follows: cut a strip of ordinary masking tape about a half inch wide and as long as the sole of your 5 or 6 iron. Go to your driving range and hit about 10 shots of the plastic mat. Yes, that's right, I did say the plastic mat. This is the only time the plastic mat can be useful to you.

Now look at the bottom of your club. If you are coming into the ball correctly at impact, the tape will be evenly scrapped off the sole of the club. If the heal is scrapped off, but the toe is still in tact, then a standard lie clubhead angle is not going to work for you. If the opposite is true with the heal of the club, then again a standard lie will not work.

Golf Above the Shoulders – Little things to enhance your game

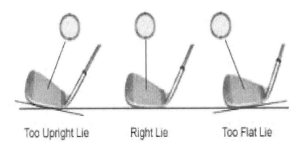

Too Upright Lie   Right Lie   Too Flat Lie

If your toe is up in the air, you need a club with a "flat lie". Club heads can be bent from 1 to 3 degrees either flat or upright to fix this problem. You will now have to talk to your Pro about getting a set of irons with flat or upright lies. I personally use irons that are 3 degrees flat.

The next item to think about is called **offset**. Offset refers to how much the bottom edge of the clubface is set back from the shaft when you look down the club. See the illustration below.

Golf Above the Shoulders – Little things to enhance your game

Offset like this is good for the average player who has a tendency to fade or slice the ball. Most sets incorporate this offset into their standard models to different degrees. You will need to hit shots with demo clubs to decide how much offset you are comfortable with.

The next club head characteristic to think about is called **bounce**. This refers to the width of the sole of the club head and the angle the leading edge makes with the ground (flat surface). In the illustration below, "A" refers to the bounce angle which

Golf Above the Shoulders – Little things to enhance your game

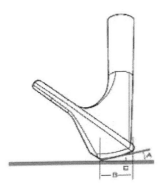

shows the leading edge of the club head is elevated in reference to the green ground line. Bounce has always been part of the characteristics of sand irons because with the leading edge up a little bit, the club head rides along the surface more that digging in. Some manufacturers are now incorporating more bounce into all of the irons, not just the sand clubs. For many players this is a great idea because it will cut down on "fat" shots, or at least minimize the amount of "fatness" on your bad hits. I also like the idea of a little more mass low on the club head for the longer irons.

So, after you improve your mechanics with a few golf lessons and are ready for a nice new set of clubs, make sure you discuss with your Pro the points we have discussed in this section:

Lie – Most important;
Offset – Can help with a slice
Bounce – Can help with consistency

The Truth about Shafts

You, no doubt, have heard and read a lot of information about shafts, and flexes, and materials, etc. It gets very technical and can be confusing.

What I am about to discuss in this section is my opinion based on my own experiences and experiments I have done over the years with many different types of shaft materials, lengths, kick points, and flexes. Your golf pro may disagree with some of my comments, but my conclusions are based on the results of experimentation. I have done the homework!

First, let's define some terms.
Flex – Everyone knows what flex means in terms of a golf shaft. It is the amount the shaft will bend during a swing.

Golf Above the Shoulders – Little things to enhance your game

Above are some high-speed photos of real power hitters to show what the shaft is doing during a swing sequence. The pictures speak for themselves.

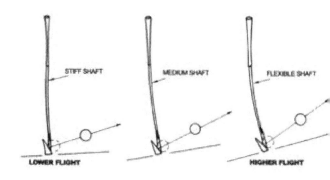

Kick Point – The kick point is the position on the shaft where the shaft will flex forward on the downswing just before impact as it reaches the lowest point of the arc.

Golf Above the Shoulders – Little things to enhance your game

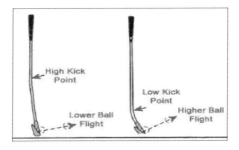

A high kick point will produce a lower trajectory while a low kick point will produce a higher trajectory.

Torque – The amount the shaft will twist off the perpendicular to the arc of the swing.

Length – The length of the shaft is self-explanatory.

Weight – This weight refers to the overall weight of the shaft which varies with the material the shaft is made from.

Now, the question is: Just how important are these shaft characteristics to a person shooting in the 80's or 90's?

As we discussed in the equipment section, they are second order correction to a faulty swing, but can have some significant effects on someone who has a good grasp on the fundamentals and wants to fine tune their shot making.

Let's take **torque** first. There isn't too much to say about torque in a golf shaft these days since modern technology has pretty much eliminated the torque problems of the early days of graphite materials.

Kick point is a shaft characteristic for a better ball striker. The average player should always chose a low kick point (if the question even arises), to get a little extra help from the shaft for getting a higher trajectory.

A better, stronger player may want a lower launch angle and let the ball rise by itself. A high kick point will allow a stronger player to do more with the trajectory when it is desirable to do so for certain shots that may require a lower launch angle.

The **length** of the club is determined by measuring the distance from the wrist, or top of the thumb joint to the ground. If you are short or tall, your pro may add or subtract ½ inch to your club length, but for most players the manufactures standard club length is suitable. Rather than fool around with club length, you will usually be better off to adjust the **lie** of the club as we discussed above.

When the club is shortened, you lose some swing speed, and when the club is longer than standard, you will struggle with accuracy due to some loss of control.

A shorter player may benefit from a flatter lie, lie 3 degrees flat instead of a shorter club length. A taller player may want to use a 3 degree upright lie instead of going longer.

Flex is a misunderstood characteristic of the club shaft. Most of the average golfers I have played with over the years believed they needed a stiff flex because they believed they generated too much club head speed for a regular flex.

Actually, an average player shooting in the high 80's and 90's or higher and hitting drives of 220 to 240 yards would get the most benefit from a regular flex shaft. They would get a little extra kick from the shaft that they would not get from a stiff flex. This is true of the woods and hybrids. The irons are a different story.

Here is a little illustration you can try. Take a pencil and break it in half. Easy, right? Now take that half and break it again. Not so easy this time. If you succeeded in breaking the half in half, then try to break it again. This time it is impossible to break because it is too short.

This principle applies to the irons. Many players like the feel of a stiff shaft for their irons, but again a regular flex will work just fine because the shorter the shaft length, the stiffer the shaft becomes naturally. Regular flex shafts will give that stiff feel with the shorter irons anyway, so you don't need to have stiff flex shafts in your irons. Of course, you can get the stiff flex for that feel in the irons, but you might lose the benefit of the extra flex in the longer irons that can help you hit higher shots.

If you are hitting drives 240 yards or longer, then you will want to use a stiffer flex. If you are generating enough speed to hit it that far, then you have the power to flex a stiffer shaft. The bottom line is that you want to get that kick from the shaft through the hitting zone and the only way to do that is to have a flex that matches your swing speed and feel. Once again your PGA Pro can advise you on the proper flex for your swing.

Now we come to weight. The weight refers to the overall weight of the club. Clubs used to be measured by "swingweight" with a range of D0 to D4 as the average swingweight for men's clubs where D0 is the lightest and D4 and higher are heavier swingweights. We don't need to discuss the details of how swingweight is measures because it is less important in todays' clubs. It had to do with the overall weight of the club and its' center of gravity. Higher swingweights felt more head heavy in your hands.

Nowadays, you don't have to be concerned with swingweight, just the overall weight of the club. Titanium drivers with graphite or thin-walled, tapered shafts weight only a few ounces and allow you to maximum your swing speed. See the next section for the physics behind energy transfer from the club to the ball. You will see why lighter clubs are more beneficial than heavier clubs.

Regarding graphic vs. thin-walled steel as shaft materials, I believe it is a matter of personal preference as to how the club feels in your hands. You will need to hit at least 10 shot with each type of shaft before choosing the type of shaft you want in a new set of clubs. Conventional wisdom put graphite in women's and senior's clubs. The idea was to concentrate more mass of the overall club in the head and less higher up in the club. In other words, the center of mass was lower in graphite clubs. The physics of this concept says something different. Without getting too scientific here, I will only say that the golf swing is a simple fulcrum. Maximum speed is generated as the center of mass gets closer to the hands and farther from the clubhead. Lighter materials in clubheads provide for that higher center of mass, and hence more swing speed. The next section will make this clearer.

So, basically, you want to use the lightest clubs to generate maximum swing speed.

Feel is a personal choice that depends only upon how the club feels in your hands. With the proper grip (which is beyond the scope of this book), you should be able to "feel" the club head when you hold the club. If you can't, you are gripping too tight. You can adjust your grip pressure and get the feel of the club in your waggle, discussed in another section. Since the grip is the only thing between you and the club, be sure your grip is correct. There are countless books, articles and internet information about the types of grips and their advantages and disadvantages. The best way to find the optimum grip for your hands and swing is to experiment with different grips. Remember, as with anything new, give it time. Whenever you are working on something new, you need to give it time for your body to adjust to the change. You will start out hitting some bad shots but don't give up right away. Look for trends of improvement in your shots. Hit at least 100 shots before you decide if the change is making any improvements. If it is, then hit 1000 more shots to perfect it! Golf is a game of persistence and patience.

Golf Above the Shoulders – Little things to enhance your game

The Proper Size Grip

GRIP SIZE IS TOO SMALL — The two middle fingers are digging into the heel portion of the golfer's palm.

GRIP SIZE IS CORRECT — The two middle fingers are slightly gapped to touching the heel portion of the golfer's palm.

GRIP SIZE IS TOO LARGE — The two middle fingers have too much gap to the heel portion of the golfer's palm.

The picture above indicates how to determine the proper grip size for the size of your hands. Grip size is important because it affects the amount of wrist activity during the swing. If the grip circumference is too large, your proper hand rotation will be reduces causing a "blocked" swing where the hands do not properly rotate through the impact area.

A grip too small actually causes the opposite, resulting in "flipping" the hands through impact. For 80% of golfers, the standard grip size is fine. If you have hands smaller or larger than the average, it makes sense to have a PGA professional check out the proper grip size for you.

In the next section we will discuss how to put new grips on your clubs. It is possible to build the grips up a little by adding one or two extra layers of the double-sided tape increasing the circumference of the grip by up to 1/16 of an inch.

Smaller or larger grips can be purchased at most golf supply stores.

How to Put Grips on a Club

The grips on your clubs will begin to dry out after about two years regardless of how much you play. When the grips are dried out, more hand and grip pressure is required to hold the club and keep it under control. The tighter you hold a club, the more your hand movement will be restricted during the swing. The result will be a lower swing speed and possibly blocked hand movement through impact.

You should replace your grips every two or three years. The cost of a grip ranges from $3.50 to $10.00. The usual charge by someone to replace the grip is in the range of $5 to $8 per grip. To save a significant amount of money when replacing the grips is to do it yourself. It is easy to do, contrary to what many people think. You will get a lot of satisfaction and feel a personal connection with your clubs.

There are two ways to re-grip a golf club; the first way is by using equipment that you can purchase, and the other way is to just use simple tools you already have around the house. If you are only going to re-grip your own set of clubs every two or three years, you don't need to buy a lot of special equipment. If you want to make some extra side money gr-gripping clubs for your friends, then buying some extra equipment will make the process a little easier and quicker. I have been regripping clubs for many years without fancy equipment because the process is so simple.

Here is what you will need to put on a new grip:

- Utility Knife like a carpet knife
- The New Grip
- Double-sided grip tape
- Solvent
- Plastic cup

The first step is to go to a golf retailer and pick out the new grips you want. There will be many types of grips from many different manufacturers. You will find rubber "wrapped" grips to all-weather cord grips and specialized putter grips. Most of the time, you will not be replacing your putter grip as often as you replace the grips on your other clubs. There are many colors also. The one that works for you is the one that feels good and has eye appeal.

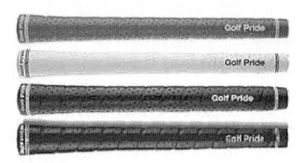

When you buy the new grips, you will need to get a roll of gripping tape and a bottle of solvent. Retailers that sell grips will also have the tape and solvent too. Pro Shops that sell grips usually do not sell the tape and solvent because they want to put the grips on for you at a charge. You can also use acetone as a solvent, but it is smelly and dries out your skin.

A bottle of solvent will be enough for a whole set of clubs or more, depending on how efficiently you use the solvent, and a roll of tape will do several sets of clubs. Shown in the picture above are the basic supplies needed to regrip a club. The picture shows pre-cut strips of double sided tape. I prefer to use a roll of tape and cut each strip to the desired length which is about ¾ the length of the grip. The pre-cut strips are longer than needed and usually only come as a set to do one set of clubs. Pre-cut tape cost more than a roll.

You can also purchase a little rubber device to hold the club in a vice while you slip on the new grip. It protects the shaft from being dented or scratched by the vice. Personally, I do not use this device, nor a vice to slip on the new grip. It just adds more time. I simply push the club head against a wall and slip the grip over the top of the shaft.

The next step is to remove the old grips using the carpet knife. Be careful to remove only the grip and not a few fingers with it.

There will be some residue on the shaft from the old tape. Clean it up a little bit. It doesn't have to be perfectly clean.

Next, cut a piece of gripping tape that is about ¾ the length of the new grip. Going lengthwise, wrap the tape round the shaft with the sticky side on the shaft. Very important – leave ½ inch of tape extending above the top of the shaft as shown.

Fold the ½ inch extended tape down over the top of the shaft and stick it onto the shaft. Now peal off the tape backing to expose the other sticky side of the tape.

You are ready to put on the new grip. Hold the grip in one hand so that finger is covering the little hole on the top of the grip. With the other hand, squirt solvent into the grip filling it to the top. Still holding the grip with the hole covered, take the club in the other hand and hold the tape end over the cup.

Golf Above the Shoulders – Little things to enhance your game

Starting at the top of the tape, as shown, pour the solvent out of the grip and onto the tape so that it runs down over the whole length of tape. The only reason for the cup is to catch the solvent so you can use it again on the next grip. You do not have to save it, just let it run into a sink if you do not want to recycle the solvent.

You are now ready to slide the grip onto the shaft. This is the only tricky part and after you do one or two grips you will see how easy it is.

You have to work quickly and smoothly. As soon as you have the grip started on the top of the shaft, use both hands to slide the grip down the rest of the way in one continuous motion. Do not make any hesitations as you slide the grip down.

Finally, align any markings that might belong on the tip side of the grip with the club face by looking down the grip and into the sole edge of the clubface. Twist the grip as needed until it is straight with the front edge of the club head.

The grip will be ready to use in about 30 minutes.

Golf Above the Shoulders – Little things to enhance your game

The Confidence of Clean Clubs

This probably really sounds silly to say that clean clubs give the feeling of confidence- but it's true. Clean clubs really do give you confidence about your ability to hit the ball. When the grooves in the clubface of your irons and fairway woods (metals), are dirty and filled with dirt, your eye/body will compensate with what, subconsciously, it thinks it needs to do. You generally will swing harder without realizing because your hand-eye coordination is telling you that you need to do something different to get the ball in the air and at the proper distance for that club. Secondly, you begin to think about the dirty clubface. It is right there in your view as you take address.

Instead of your pre-shot routine, you will be distracted.

Your subconscious will try to compensate for the dirty grooves and swing differently to get the backspin and trajectory you are looking for.

Finally, dirt-filled grooves really do present a problem for backspin. The grooves will not do the job they are supposed to do when they are filled with dirt and blend in with the surface of the clubface. Groves are very important and essential to imparting the correct amount of backspin that helps your ball to stop when it hits the green and also to give the ball the proper trajectory in flight. You probably have heard about the differences between "V" grooves and "square" groves. Each type of grove does something slightly different to the ball flight and hold characteristics.

The "V" groove was the traditional groove for golf clubs. When the sharp edged "square" groove was introduced, it added more backspin to the ball and allowed the ball to maintain backspin even out of the rough.

As of 1/1/10, the USGA with the agreement of the PGA, enacted a new rule prohibiting square grooves on clubs because they felt it gave an unfair advantage to shots hit from the rough- in other words, a player was not penalized enough for missing the fairway, because they could still get backspin on the ball with the square groove. The square groove was just too forgiving. The ruling bodies felt that the tour players should be relying on their shot-making ability when they miss the fairway rather than the advantage of still getting backspin on the ball when coming out of the rough.

So, since 2010, square grooves with sharp edges are illegal to use. The edges of the square grooves must be rounded as shown in the picture.

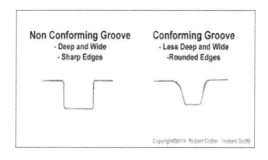

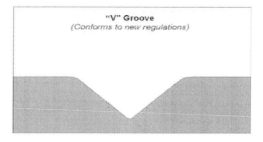

It doesn't matter which type of groove you have on your clubs if they are filled with dirt and crud!

What Ball Is Best for Your Game?

Golf balls are all pretty much made from the same materials with a solid large inner core, a thinner outer core, covered with a durable Surlyn cover. There are many brands of golf balls all making claims of increased distance, accuracy, and soft feel, etc. There are differences between ball characteristics that can have an effect on your game. So, which ball is best for you?

There are two properties of a golf ball that you need to know about in order to choose the right ball for your age, swing speed, and overall playing ability. They are compression and type of dimples.

Compression means how much a ball compresses (or how much time it remains on the clubface at impact) when hit by a golf club. Traditionally, compressions range from 70 to 100 where 70 is the softest and 100 is professional level. Manufacturers have gotten away from compression numbers on balls, but they still range from soft to hard compressions. The USGA has regulations as to compressions and ball flight velocity. The maximum allowable compressed is 2/10ths of an inch when struck. This puts a lower limit on ball softness.

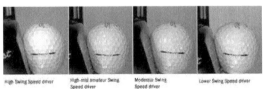

High Swing Speed driver   High-mid amateur Swing Speed driver   Moderate Swing Speed driver   Lower Swing Speed driver

If you use a ball that has a higher compression than your swing speed can compress, then you will be losing performance, and maybe distance on your longer shots. When you are able to compress the ball, it will launch off the clubface at a higher angle producing a higher shot which is desirable for maximum distance and carry. For the 80's and 90's players, a medium compression (old 80 compression number), will do just fine.

The next major characteristic of a golf ball is the dimple structure on the surface. There are basically three types of dimples with variations on all of them. There are shallow, deep and small dimples, and each type does something different.

To properly describe the differences, we may need a little science. Research into the flight of a golf ball has revealed some really interesting data. Using wind tunnels and high speed photography, and using colored smoke to make the air flow more distinctive, the exact nature of the air flow over a ball in flight with different types of spins has been exactly determined. The next step was to manipulate or control the laminar air flow over the surface of the ball by altering the structure of the dimples.

When a golf ball is in flight, it is encapsulated in a layer of air about one millimeter thick which actually produces drag on the ball as it goes through the air. If this thin layer of air can be eliminated, the ball would then be in direct contact with the fast moving air all around it as it is in flight. Hence, the science of dimple structure was born.

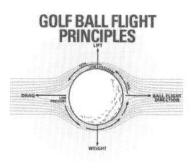

As the dimples break up that dead layer of air close to the ball, the ball is exposed to the fast air moving all around it. That fast moving air produces lift just like over an aircraft wing. Controlling the dimple depth, will control the amount of lift the ball will experience in flight.

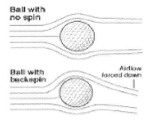

Deep dimples do the best job of breaking up that layer of static air around the ball allowing it to be exposed to the fast air moving over the surface. The result is more lift, a higher trajectory and a steeper decent. Deeper dimples will also produce greater side movement like draws and fades and may be harder to control on windy days.

Deeper dimples produce more lift and higher flight

Shallow dimples do less to break up the static layer so the trajectory is lower and more boring through the air. There is less lift so the ball will not climb up as much and will roll out more on the fairway.

Golf Above the Shoulders – Little things to enhance your game

Shallow dimples produce less lift and a lower flight.

Small dimples will inhibit draws and fades, and will not climb in flight like deeper dimples.

There are variations of these three basic dimples such as hexagonal dimples. The overall goal of these dimples is to increase the destruction of the static layer around the ball.

There are also balls with all three types incorporated on the ball. You have to decide if they play any differently for you.

It is interesting to note that driving range balls have a compression of about 45 to cut down on their distance. When you see "Range", or "Practice" printed on the ball, they will be very soft and you will not get a true measure of the distance you can hit your longer clubs. Driving range owners want to keep their practice balls inside the range and not overshoot the field. In fact, after a season of being hit hundreds of times, the balls feel like foam rubber and really do not go too far because they get softer from so much use. They are not premium balls to begin with and after being hit and compressed so many times, they are pretty useless in terms of feel and distance by the end of the season.

So how do you choose a ball that is best for your game? Here are a few simple guidelines to help you decide.

First of all, you may not want to use the same type of ball all of the time. For example, on windy days, you may want to use a harder ball with shallow dimples to minimize the climb and compression, so the ball flies lower and bores into the wind.

A general rule of thumb would be that if you have a swing speed under 90mph with a driver, you would probably do better with a softer, or lower compression ball. Swing faster than 90 mph and a harder ball would give you a little more distance.

There may be situations where a player with a higher swing speed may still want a softer ball because of its' flight characteristics and feel.

A softer ball will compress more and stay on the clubface longer. The result will be a higher launch angle and more spin. The shot will go higher, land softer and have more backspin when it hits the green. These flight characteristics may be more desirable on certain courses. Of course, since the shot will have more spin, it is prone to move left or right more and be affected by the wind more than a harder ball with a little less spin.

Remember, you cannot change a ball while playing a hole, but you can change the ball between holes. In fact, the pros play a new ball every two or three holes because they hit the ball so hard, it could go out-of-round.

THE SWING

Let's Get a Little Technical

In the previous sections, we talked a little bit about what to look for in the design of the clubhead for the irons and how they relate to your body and swing.

Then we discussed a few characteristics of shafts and how they affect your ball flight.

Now, I want to end the discussions about the physical characteristics of golf clubs with a little bit of Physics. There is much more technology to the structure of gold clubs than we have talked about, but what we have not discussed is left to the engineers that figure out how to build a better "mousetrap". I do, however want to touch on one technical point that all golfers need to understand- the transfer of energy from the clubhead to the ball.

Golf Above the Shoulders – Little things to enhance your game

$$E_k = \frac{1}{2}mv^2$$

E_k = kinetic energy of object

m = mass of object

v = speed of object

When a clubhead strikes a golf ball, kinetic energy (the energy of motion), is transferred to the ball from the clubhead. To be perfectly correct, a Physicist would modify the above equation by replacing the V with a greek omega for rotational velocity, but the form of the equation is the same.

So, what you want to do is to maximize the E_k, the kinetic energy, so that you are imparting the maximum amount of energy onto the ball. Looking at the equation, the E depends on ½ the mass of the clubhead and the square of the velocity of the clubhead. This means that the mass (hence weight) of the clubhead is rather insignificant in developing the kinetic energy to move the ball as compared to the square of the velocity, or clubhead speed generated in the swing. Any increase in clubhead speed will develop extra energy as the square of the incremental increase. That's a big payback!

I am not sure when club manufactures started applying this simple physics to golf technology, probably in the late 70's, but when they did, we started to see all of the advances in light weight materials to facilitate increasing the speed of the clubhead.

This is all the proof you need to verify that clubhead speed is the key to distance, not mass or anything else in a swing.

There are other technical details about golf equipment that are out of our control in terms of club customization, such as clubface roll. Since these items are part of the standard engineering of clubhead structure, we don't need to discuss them here. Needles to say, when scientific research was seriously applied to golf clubs, we started to see vast improvements.

Light weight shafts and titanium heads have allowed for greater distance off the tee, and have kept seniors maintaining driving distance that they would otherwise have lost in the pre-technology era.

Get your lessons, increase the consistency of your game, then go out and get a new set of clubs that fit your swing and body type and start hitting killer drives!

A Word about the Swing Plane

Although this is not a book about swing mechanics, I feel the need to say a few words about the swing plane. A lot has been written and taught about the "proper" swing plane. Conventional wisdom says the club should move back and return to the impact position from the inside. So, if you have an imaginary plane from your shoulders to the ball, your clubhead would always move underneath this plane as shown in the illustration below.

The difficulty with this, is that many people cannot accomplish this inside-out approach due to body flexibility, age, size etc. There are other swing planes that work just as well in producing excellent ball striking results.

There are variations of three basic swing plane types.

- The Inside Loop
- The Outside Loop (pictured below)
- The In-Plane swing (no loops)

The conventional way of teaching golf was to teach the inside-out swing where you take the club back in a comfortable plane (not forcing it inside), and return to the ball from the inside after dropping into the "slot" on the way down.

Golf Above the Shoulders – Little things to enhance your game

This type of swing will produce a draw, or a right to left shot for a right hand golfer. This is not easily accomplished for an average player because it requires a well-executed transition, a proper clearing of the right side, and strong legs. The picture above, shows the conventional way of teaching the swing plane. I do not fully agree with this approach since most average golfers cannot achieve this swing. Although this is picturesque, an outside-in swing can also produce successful results.

Most golfers swing with an outside-in loop as shown in the previous picture above. This type of swing will produce a left to right trajectory, or a fade for a right hander.

This swing is fine as long as you get into the slot as you return to the ball.

This type of swing can also produce a "casting" affect in returning to the ball.

Both of the pictures above show the "casting" of the club on the downswing. The picture on the left shows the top yellow line forming 90 degrees with the left arm. This is called being in the "slot" and when the club is unleashed in the hitting area, maximum clubhead speed results. In the picture, the golfers club is about 65 degrees (according to the picture) out of the slot, meaning that much of the clubhead speed has been lost in the downswing and nothing will be left in the hitting zone except what the player can muscle through. The picture on the right shows the same problem. When you return to the ball from the outside, it is easy to fall into this situation. You can avoid this from happening and still get into the slot from an outside loop but you must practice keeping the 90-degree angle between you arm and the shaft until the hands have reached near the bottom of the swing. Practicing in from of a mirror will help you get the feel of this, but the best fix is to see a PGA Professional who can take a video of your swing, play it slow for you to see, and help you with the proper fix.

With the proper release of the club, you should be able to hit the ball about ¾ of the full distance with just ½ the swing. If you can do this, then you have a proper delay. If not, see your local pro for help.

Golf Above the Shoulders – Little things to enhance your game

This may be a good casting form to catch a fish, but it certainly does not work on a golf course

The Swing Thought

If there is only one thing you take away from this book, it should be the idea of having a swing thought. I cannot over emphasize the power and importance of having a consistent swing thought. A mental feeling and or vision of something that makes it all come together for you. When I spoke of my 10-year old daughter progressing quickly into the game, I have to attribute her early success to her developing and understanding the importance of having an effective and consistent swing thought.

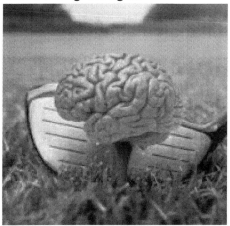

Now, what exactly is a swing thought? It is a visualization or a feeling of something about your swing or ball flight that makes you forget about specific mechanics and allows you to concentrate on the "whole" of your swing execution. It is the single most important factor in taking what you have learned at the practice tee to the first tee of the course. It helps you to swing consistently on every shot during your round.

Every Tour player, 100%, has a swing thought and you need one too.

I can tell you what a swing thought is not; it is not a single specific detail of your swing that you have been working on, or think you should try while playing. You should not be thinking about a new grip you are trying or trying to get your left shoulder under your chin, or anything else like that. Those items you work on at the practice tee. Trust your muscles to remember, and never replace your swing thought with mechanical details.

A swing thought will help you NOT to think about HOW you are doing WHAT you are doing when you are playing well. We all do this at some time or another- we start off a round with 3 pars, or a couple of pars and a birdie, and then start second-guessing why we are playing so well when we "know" we are bogy golfers. This type of thought pattern will guarantee that you will return to bogy golf! You are just having a good day. Everything is clicking; the mechanics, the turn, the timing, etc. If you maintain your consistent swing thought, you may extend your success to a few more holes. If you try to analyze your success, you will pick out some detail (which will probably not be the actual reason everything is working together), and start concentrating on it. The result is always disastrous and you will lose your momentum.

A swing thought is any thought that you can consistently think about each time you are ready to swing the club. It has to be the same each time you are ready to make a full shot (excludes putting and chipping). Over the years, my swing thought has been more like a feeling of a plane that I must swing under as I take the club back. This thought or feeling makes me stay in plane, gives me good rhythm and keeps me on the inside with a one-piece takeaway. That one thought keeps me doing all of these things without thinking about any one of them individually.

It will take you some time to develop your individual thought and you will have to modify it as you go, but you must work on developing your unique trigger that makes everything come together. It does not have to be a golf related idea either. I knew a pro that used to think of his red Ford Mustang convertible before he began his swing. He did not want to slip into thinking about mechanical specifics. It worked for him.

Golf Above the Shoulders – Little things to enhance your game

Lining up at Address

Here is another item that sounds obvious but one that most average golfers overlook- their setup over the ball. It really is simple and there is no excuse to be improperly aligned before you swing.

The setup should be part of your pre-shot routine. You start with your feet and work your way up. Feet in the correct position for the shot you want to hit. The knees slightly bent in an athletic position with inward pressure on the right knee (for right hand golfers- left knee for left hand players). Next align the hips and shoulders to be parallel to the line of flight. It is a natural tendency to line up "open" at address because of the way the human body is constructed. In the beginning you may have to make a conscience effort to line up "square" or parallel to the line of flight. After a while it will be automatic, but you still need to make the lineup part of your pre-shot routine.

There are always exceptions to the general rule, such as Lee Trevino who always lined up open and took the club back on the outside. Lee recovered by dropping perfectly into the slot on the way down and was one of the most solid ball strikers ever to play.

Lining Up the Clubface

Making solid contact with the ball is the goal of every shot. Making contact with the ball on the center of mass of the clubface requires precision in your swing and this starts with the proper lineup at address. The center of mass on the clubface is also called the sweet spot. It is the point on the face where all of the mass seems to be concentrated at impact. Anywhere off the center of mass will produce a torque proportional to the distance off center. While torque is good for your car, it is bad for your shot.

Hitting the sweet spot on the clubface starts with the proper alignment at address. However lining up the ball with the sweetspot at address does not necessarily guarantee you will make contact with the center of mass when you actually swing and hit the ball. There are variations in all golf swings and a proper clubface alignment for one player may not work for another. Through practice, you have to find the proper address alignment that will produce contact with the center of mass when you actually hit the ball- there are variations in all swings.

Most clubs have a little mark indicating where the center of mass can be found. You should use that mark to adjust your alignment at setup that best suits your swing. For example, when I line up my driver at address, I position the little indicator on the top of the driver with the far side of the ball. I do not line up the club indicator with the center of the ball, but rather with the perimeter of the ball that is farthest from me. This will increase my chances of hitting the proper spot on the clubface when I make contact.

I never had a chance to see Billy Casper play when he was on the regular tour, but I saw him several times on the Senior Tour. When he lined up his driver, the ball was actually beyond the clubhead. No part of the golf ball was lined up with the face of the club! As he came into the hitting zone, he moved into the shot and made solid contact with the ball.

Avoid Grounding Your Club

If you have ever noticed pictures of the Tour players or seen videos or even attended a PGA Tour event you may have noticed that the players do not ground their club at address. They are holding the club head just slightly above the ground. It may not even be any higher off the ground than the short cut grass, but nevertheless, the club is not resting on the ground. They are supporting the entire weight of the club in their hands at address.

There are a couple of reasons for this. The first reason is that it gives the player a feel for the clubhead. It is a good way to establish the correct grip pressure. If your grip is too tight, you cannot feel the clubhead, the weight of the club all feels the same without feeling the clubhead at the end of the shaft. The second reason is to allow the forearms to maintain a uniform flex throughout the swing. When you ground the club, you have a tendency to tighten your grip at takeaway and therefore tightening up the muscles of the forearm. This restricts the movement of the wrists and forearms as the muscles of the forearms tighten up through the backswing. By holding the club just above the ground at address, the same pressure is maintained throughout the backswing eliminating the muscular tension of tightening forearms.

The Fast Track to Contact

I have mentioned several times now, that this is not a book about swing mechanics. However, I've seen so many golfers, especially seniors (over 50), that barely hit their drivers 150 yards. That's why I've come up with the fast track to impact idea. It consists of only 5 simple points to incorporate into your swing to get you driving the ball 200 yards consistently.
Of course, I recommend professional golf lessons, but this Fast-Track can get you started hitting the ball quicker until you get your golf lesson scheduled.
There are many great videos and books produced by noted teachers, many of which are teachers and coaches to the Tour players. I recommend that you take advantage of this information but a lot of it is very technical and may seem to be overwhelming to you.
So, try this simple Fast Track to Impact method to get you making better contact with the ball. I will list the five points and then describe each one in a little more detail. At the end of this book, you will find additional detail for each point and the

rationale behind them for those of you that need this detail.

#1 - The right knee
#2 - The shaft angle
#3 - The swing thought
#4 – Balance
#5 – Trust Your Swing

You will notice that of the five points above, three are physical, and two are mental. You cannot achieve a successful golf swing without a solid mental image of what you are trying to do.

#1: the Right Knee
What you're going to do with your right knee occurs only at set up and then you can forget about it.
When you take your address to the ball, you have your weight evenly distributed on both feet, with perhaps a little favor toward your left foot. Once set up, apply some inward pressure on your right knee. You do this without moving your hips or twisting your hips or any other part of your body, just a slight inward pressure of your right knee toward the middle of your stance and this will put the weight on your right foot

more on your instep rather than on the full bottom of your foot. Maintain this pressure throughout the backswing.

#2 - the shaft angle
This step is very important. You want to imagine the angle of your shift to be about 45° with the ground when using the driver. You need to maintain this angle as you go back through your backswing, and as you return the club in your downswing.

#3 - The Proper Swing Thought
In the previous section on swing thought, I told you that it was a personal thought that you developed to make your swing work. Now, as the third point of the Fast Track, I'm going to tell you what your swing thought needs to be.

In this case, your swing thought needs to be a visualization of your shaft angle throughout your swing. So in other words, the mechanics of point number two is now your mental visualization for point number three.

You will establish this visualization at set up, and maintain it throughout your swing. Never start your swing until your swing thought is your main focus with no other distracting thoughts.

#4; Balance

It is extremely important to maintain balance throughout the entire swing. You do whatever it takes in your swing to maintain your balance. It will force you to swing slower and smoother. No more trying to muscle the ball which results in casting from the top and losing all of your swing speed.

#5: Trust Your Swing

If you do not trust that your swing will perform for you, that it will generate the speed you need to make a decent shot, you will force the downswing, or swing back too quickly, or make many other errors trying to engineer each shot.

The engineering is for the practice tee. When you are on the course, you MUST trust your swing basics. You MUST believe that your swing will give you the proper results. You should only be focused on your swing thought, maintain your balance, and you will see amazing, consistent results.

To make this Fast Track method work, you have to develop it at the practice tee. Go to the driving range, get a bucket of balls and start to employ each point in the order they are listed.

Start with the inward pressure of the right knee. You will mess up a lot of shots until you get the feeling, but it will begin to improve your contact by slowly eliminating fat shots, and improving your transition in the start of the downswing.

Next, after you feel comfortable with the right knee pressure, you will start to visualize your shaft angle going back and coming through the ball.

The Transition

The "transition" definitely involves mechanics, which is not the intention of this book, however I want to point it out to you to be aware of the importance of a good transition.

Above is a swing sequence of Sam Snead. Although the exact point of Transition is not shown, the results shown in picture 1 to picture 2 shows Snead "in the slot" in picture 2 as his club and hands drop and his elbow is close to his body. This was the source of his tremendous power and speed generation.

The transition is the split-second portion of your backswing when you finish going back and start down into the ball. It is intimately related to your weight shift. Sometimes with some people, they can get an idea of how to move their weight forward by have a good vision of the transition portion of their swing.

Golf Above the Shoulders – Little things to enhance your game

Another great golfer, Ben Hogan. Again as in the Snead photos, you can see Hogan's hands have dropped into the slot, weight transferred (look at his knees), and elbow close to his body.

Good weight transfer will cause a good transition which will result in the club "dropping into the slot". This generates your clubhead speed. Check this out with some books on mechanics.

These pictures of Jack Nicklaus do show the point of Transition at the top of the swing where there is not much body motion, however a lot is happening. His weight is moving forward, his club and hands are dropping into the slot, his knees are driving forward, he is pushing off his right side using his massive leg muscles of the upper right leg, and his hips have begun rotation. Jack could generate huge amounts of power and speed.

The Hitting Zone

The final majorly important physical aspect of the golf swing is the Hitting Zone. The proper backswing, swing tempo, and transition all set up for what happens in the hitting zone. It is this area of the swing where the clubhead makes contact with the ball and transfers kinetic energy from clubhead to ball. We discussed earlier that clubhead speed (kinetic energy) is what generates the power. When this energy is transferred to the ball, the ball is slightly compressed and flys off the clubface. It makes sense then, that you want to generate the maximum amount of clubhead speed possible. Maximum speed is a result of tempo, flexibility and swing coordination rather than brute power. In fact, swinging hard is usually counter-productive for the average payer. The pros know how to swing harder when they need to, but for the rest of us, it will usually cause a loss of distance.

The picture below is the best way to describe why the hitting zone is so important. In this picture of Sam Snead, we can see how clubhead speed is generated. The hands move along the yellow path in the same amount of time the clubhead moves along the red path. You can see the speed of the hands is multiplied by the length of the club shaft. The key to the "delay" is in the 90 degree angle made between the left arm and the club shaft as the club enters the hitting zone (right handed players, opposite for left hand players). When you try to swing hard, this angle is lost and so is all of your speed. There are many sequential photos available in books and on the internet. Check them out and you will see all of the pros with this move. It is basic. See the section on the "Tempo Drill" to practice how to achieve this.

The Waggle

Most players use a waggle of some form. A waggle is the action or movement you make at address just before you hit the ball. The waggle serves a few purposes.

It allows you to feel the clubhead and establish the correct grip pressure with your hands. Not too tight, not too loose. Like holding a baby bird, as Sam Snead put it.

The waggle gives you a sense of rhythm for the swing. You can't move the club smoothly if your grip is too tight and your forearms too tense. Tense forearms translate into restricted hand and wrist release through the hitting zone resulting in loss of clubhead speed. The speed of your waggle should echo the speed of your takeaway and backswing.

Golf Above the Shoulders – Little things to enhance your game

Finally, it can help you focus and concentrate on hitting the ball.

The Pre-Shot Routine

I have previously said that the Swing Thought was the single most important thing to take away from this book. Some players might argue that the pre-shot routine is the most important thing to remember. I can see their point, because the pre-shot routine is what brings it all together. All of the items we are discussing culminate in the pre-shot routine. Just like a Swing Thought, you HAVE to have a beginning routine that never varies from shot to shot. I would even venture to say that it should be the same for putts and chips too. Again, like the swing thought, it is your personal creation- can be short, like Lee Trevino, or longer like Sergio Garcia. Every Tour player has a pre-shot routine. It gets them focused on the shot, eliminates environmental distractions, and calms them down by eliminating the pressure of the moment. You will focus all of your attention on your pre-shot routine and eliminate outside distractions or feelings of inability or lack of confidence.

Golf Above the Shoulders – Little things to enhance your game

The pre-shot routine is so important that good players and Tour players will start their routine all over if they are distracted as they go through it. Good players also have a pre-shot process for putting too. It is not just limited to full shots. The putting routine may be quite different from a full shot, but nevertheless, they have one.

I will go through my pre-shot routine as an example:

- It starts with teeing the ball up. I put the ball in the ground deliberately to make sure I have the correct tee height for the club I will be using.
- Then I step the grass down behind the ball with my right foot. I don't know exactly why I do this, except that I do. It is probably a throwback from my younger days when I sometimes played

on some pretty bad golf courses where grass was scarce!
- Next, I step back about 10 feet behind the ball and look down the fairway for a target to hit to. Prior to teeing the ball, I had decided on a strategy on how I am going to play the hole. When I pick out the target, I look for a spot about 3 feet in front of the ball to use to align myself up at address. When I line up to that spot I will be exactly aligned to the target I want to hit in the fairway.
- While still behind the ball, I take a short swing to get the rhythm
- I move up to the ball for address and get the grip on the club. Then place the club head behind the ball aligned with the spot I picked out 3 feet in front of the ball.
- Next I place my right foot, then my left foot (I am right handed) and relax my knees.
- Next I square my hips to avoid the usual mistake many people make of leaving the hips and shoulders open at address. Finally I make sure my shoulders are square to the target line. (Note: Sometimes I want to stand open,

in that case, I make sure my feet, hips, and shoulders are all aligned parallel)
- By this time I am totally oblivious to the surroundings and am ready for the last thing to do, which is to get the swing thought.
- As I am settling in on the swing thought, I will do one or two waggles. I don't have a reason for why it is one or two, it just is, depending on how I feel, I guess.
- I am ready to swing. I will not start the swing however, until I have the swing thought in place.

You may be saying by now, "OMG, what a slow player!". Actually this whole routine takes less than 90 seconds, but it is enough time filled with enough activities to allow me to focus on the shot and eliminate disruptive and counterproductive thoughts.

Golf Above the Shoulders – Little things to enhance your game

Know Your Game, Trust Your Swing

This section deals with understanding your limitations and strong points to achieve the lowest scores possible for you. To know your game is to understand what you do best and where your challenges are and then playing the percentages on those strong and weak points.

You need to know your distances with each club, and where your gaps may be in yardage. Maybe the greatest "percentage" player of all time was Jack Nicklaus. He knew what he could do, and always chose the shot that would give him the greatest odds of being successful. He played the percentages and if the shot did not come off exactly as planned, he was never too far off for a recovery shot to follow.

Many people over the years have criticized Arnold Palmer for taking too many chances with recovery shots that were too risky. Maybe sometimes he did and that created part of his legend, however, he knew his game, he knew his physical strength and knew he could maneuver the ball. Many of the shots he was able to hit that dazzled us, were not lucky shots at all, they were shots that he knew he could make. Shots he practiced over and over. He also would choose the shot that had the greatest odds of success, except for him, his odds were quite different that a lot of the other players!

Knowing your game combined with the ideas in the section on selecting your target will put you closer to the pin on your approach shots than you probably get now.

Specifically, you need to know the distance you hit each club, how high the average shot will get in the air and if it fades or draws. In other words, you need to know your distance and trajectory for each club in your bag.

When you know how you hit each club, then you need to use that information when deciding how to play each shot. Your confidence will go way up as you stand over the ball. The shot you play may not always be the glamorous choice, or the one you would see on TV, but it won't be a wasted shot either.

When you have a solid swing thought, and you trust your swing, you can eliminate the self-doubt that will always ruin your game.

Too many golfers play the text-book shot; the one they think they are supposed to play. If they have 150 yards to the hole slightly up hill, they will hit a 7-iron because that is the club they think they are supposed to use for that distance. But what about the other factors like slightly up hill, or the pin in the back- these two items alone could add two club-lengths to the shot. When they hit a good shot, most golfers will end up on the front edge of the green. It happens 80% of the time. Rarely do you see an 80's or 90's player get their second shot back to the hole.

Once your have selected your club and shot strategy, it is time for your pre-shot routine. **At this point it is time to TRUST YOUR SWING.** You have the proper club, you know how you want to play the hole, so all you have to do is execute. As I have said earlier, NEVER think about how you are doing what you are doing. Just get your swing thought in place and swing with 80% power and let it happen. You will find that most of the time it WILL happen for you. If you have doubt, or think you are trying something that has little chance of success. Then step away from the ball and re-evaluate what you are doing. Don't worry if you are taking too much time. The extra 2 minutes getting the correct club and shot, will be a far shorter time than will result from a bad shot in the trees that will take 10 minutes to find the ball!

Putting It All Together

I hope you have enjoyed this information and use this little book as a reference on a regular basis to get the most from your golf experiences.

I would say that the most important sections would be the concept of having a swing thought, (page 61), a pre-shot routine, (page 95), and Knowing your game and trusting your swing, (page 127).

If there is nothing else you take away from this book, it is those items. Incorporate them into every shot you make and you will start to see improvements in the way you play, in your consistency, in your score, and in your overall enjoyment of the game.

Golf Above the Shoulders – Little things to enhance your game

Golf Above the Shoulders – Little things to enhance your game

COURSE MANAGEMENT AND STRATEGY

Plan a Strategy for each Hole

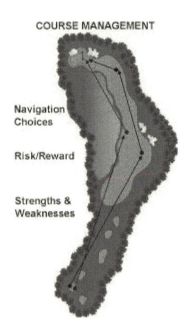

Planning on how you are going to play the hole before you actually play it is fun and exciting. It gives your round of golf more validity and gets you into your round. Even if your skill level is not so good, you should still have a play book for each hole.

You don't have to do this in advance of going to the course (unless you want to). You can actually develop your strategy as

Copyright 2017 All Rights Reserved

you stand on the tee waiting for your playing partners to tee off. Basically, you should be visualizing where you want your tee shot to land to optimize your next shot. You should be one shot ahead in your thinking. If you are not confident that you can hit the spot, you should still have one selected (see the section on picking out a target). There is always the chance that you will place the ball where you planned and it will give you a lot of satisfaction.

As you look down the fairway of a par 4, for example, look for traps around the green if you can see them. If you don't know the course, ask you playing partners if they know what is ahead on the hole. You can take hazards out of play if you have a target strategy to avoid them. It will increase you enjoyment regardless of your skill level. Just remember to make your strategy attainable for your skill level. If you know you cannot reach a particular par 5 in three, then plan to get there in four shots with a one-putt. If you miss the putt, then at least you will get the bogey which is better than expecting to hit the green in regulation and as a result swinging like a mad-man. That is surely the way to waste strokes.

One of my friends is a little worse than average; shoots about 100. Yet every shot he lines up to hit, he expects to have Tour-quality results. As a result he is constantly frustrated, even when he makes a good shot for his skill level. If he used a strategy, he would be happy when he hit a shot as planned and would actually cut about 5 or more strokes off his score.\

So, the bottom line is to have a realistic strategy on how you want to play each hole and you will get a lot more fun and satisfaction out of each round (after all, it is just a game).

Selecting Your Target

Properly selecting your target is important for good shot making, focus and concentration. You must always have a target picked out before you hit the ball. Selecting you target should be part of your strategy and pre-shot routine.

The target you select, should be a very precise and specific location. It could be a spot on the fairway or something in the distant background of the hole. The point is that it must be small and specific, not just aiming at the fairway or green. It is much easier for the brain to focus on a small target rather than a large area. If you miss a small target, there is a better chance of keeping the ball in play. If you miss a fairway, well, you know what happens.

Examples of specific targets could be the "left edge of a fairway trap", or "the trunk of a pine tree behind the green". When you select where you want to aim, you hold that image in your mind as your focal point for line-up. It also could be part of your swing thought too. Just stay focused on it.

When choosing a target you also have to consider the distance you need to hit the ball, too. If you choose a distant target, you are getting direction only. You will also need to determine the distance you need to carry as well as wind conditions so you can hit your spot.

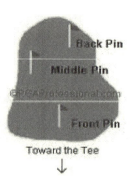

When hitting to a green, you will need two distances, the distance to the front of the green and the distance to the flag. These distances may not be easy to determine.

GPS apps are free to most cell phones and can help greatly in determining approach distances. Many of the Tour players use three distances; distance to the front of the green, distance to the pin, and distance to the back of the green.

These distances "box" in the green for proper club selection. The average golfer hits to the front of the green most of the time without getting the ball back to the pin. It is a visual thing- seeing the front of the green and selecting a club to get there. The pin placement on a normal-sized green could be one or two club lengths longer than just getting to the front. Many courses use some sort of indicator on the actual flag stick like a red or white plastic ball. When it is high on the stick, the hole is near the back of the green, when low it is near the front. When you see that the pin is toward the back of the green, always use one club longer to get the ball back to the hole and increase your chance of a one putt green.

Golf Above the Shoulders – Little things to enhance your game

Analyze the Wind Velocity

The wind factor can completely change the characteristics of a golf course and the way you play. Part of your playing strategy for each hole is to analyze the wind conditions. It seems like the wind is always blowing in your face regardless of the direction of the hole! You need to be aware of head wind, trailing wind and cross wind because each on these directions will have a different impact on your distance and trajectory.

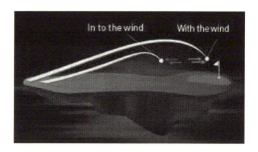

Tom Watson was, and still is, a master at playing in adverse weather conditions and high winds, hence 5 British Opens- an amazing accomplishment. He practiced in adverse conditions before the tournament in order to have his game tuned for the Open. Don't be afraid to be creative with your shot-making when the wind is howling in your face.

A head wind will shorten your shot and cause the ball to rise and drop shorter than normal. You have to get a feel for a 1-club wind, a 2-club wind, etc. A 1-club wind means simply that you need to use one club longer; 2-club means 2 clubs longer, etc. I really don't have a rule-of-thumb for the number of clubs longer vs. wind speed because it depends on the trajectory of your normal shots. If you usually hit a low ball, you may not need to club longer as much as a person that hits a higher normal shot. It also depends on how strong you are as a hitter. The things to be aware of is that 1). It is a head wind, 2). Your shot will rise and travel shorter, 3). Any side spin your ball has- like draw or fade, will be exacerbated travelling into the wind and could turn into a hook or slice, respectively.

Golf Above the Shoulders – Little things to enhance your game

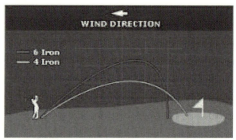

In this illustration, we are looking at a 2-club head wind.

When teeing your ball into the wind, tee it lower than usual, some players will move the ball back a little in their stance, to keep it a low flight. When you line up, you will have to focus on balance as well. Be sure to make a deliberate, maybe a little slower backswing in order to maintain balance throughout the swing. A windy condition will affect your balance and hence your ability to make solid contact.

A trailing wind will do different things to your ball flight. A trailing wind will actually straighten out your ball flight and keep it a little straighter in the wind direction. This is an opportunity to hit the shot higher to squeeze out a little more distance. The ball will not rise like a head wind and may not "bite" as effectively when it hits the green.

As far as selecting the correct club for a trailing wind, the same principle applies in reverse to a head wind. You may have to club shorter with a trailing wind and the ball will usually run a bit more on the green or fairway.

Side winds can be tricky. If a side wind is blowing in the direction of how your ball normally curves, the curve will be exaggerated by the side wind. If you ball usually curves into the direction of the side wind, it may straighten out, but will fly a shorter distance. You will have to make your best guess about which club to use and how much distance you will lose. At least if you try to compensate for the wind, you will have a better chance of success than if you just ignore the wind.

Golf Above the Shoulders – Little things to enhance your game

Hitting to Different Elevations

Many approach shots will be to greens that are either elevated above the fairway, or are below the level of the fairway. You will need to assess the elevation differences based on the normal trajectory of your shots in order to determine which club to use. For elevated greens, you will need a longer club than usual and for greens that are below the level of the fairway, you will need to use a shorter club. The reason is due to the trajectory of the ball flight. If you look at the little drawing below, you will see that the ball trajectory to an elevated green is interrupted earlier in the flight by hitting a higher green surface, and therefore a longer club is needed to reach the green. The opposite is true for greens that are below the level of the fairway. In this case, as shown, the trajectory of the ball will carry it farther than if the green were at the same level of the fairway, hence a shorter club is required.

Golf Above the Shoulders – Little things to enhance your game

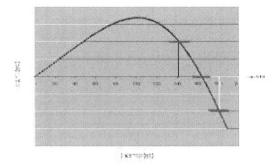

The tricky issue here, is how much do you club up or down with different elevations. There is no exact rule-of-thumb because it is based on the trajectory of your normal shots. If you traditionally hit high shots, you will not need to club up as much as someone who usually hits low shots (to an elevated green). The opposite is true in clubbing down to a lower elevation. You will just have to experiment with hitting to different elevations until you are fairly confident with your club selection based on target elevations.

The thing to remember is that you definitely will have to hit a different club than usual when the green is not close to the same elevation of the fairway. This assessment will become part of your strategy for playing the hole. Another thing to remember about strategy when playing this type of hole is where your tee shot or pre-approach shot will land prior to the shot to the higher or lower green. It is always easier (for the average player) to hit from a flat, level lie than from a down-hill or up-hill lie. If the fairway starts to slope to the different elevation, you may end up with a up or down-hill lie which will complicate the shot even more. Decide whether or not is would be better to hit a shorter shot, or to a different placement in the fairway where you would end up with a flatter or more desirable lie for that approach shot to the elevated or low lying green.

I will leave you with one final observation that I have been guilty of many times. When hitting to an elevated green where you cannot see the actual green surface, maybe only the top of the flag, be sure to take enough club to get on the green, not just on the front of the hill, and end up short. It is a visual tendency to hit for the top of the hill- or front of the green area with the result that when you get to the green, up the hill, you ended up short of the actual green surface by five yards! It is very aggravating since one club longer would have done the job and got you to the green.

You will feel the calming effects right on the course as you are playing.

Golf Above the Shoulders – Little things to enhance your game

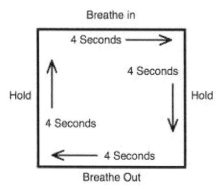

GOLF COURSE ETIQUITTE

You can find many books and articles which discuss proper behavior on a golf course, so I thought I would add my own list of the items I believe are the most important points of etiquette that we all should follow to make and keep the game enjoyable.

Golf is a social sport. We rarely play by ourselves. We always look for a playing partner or a foursome when we go out to play a round of golf. Bad behavior during the round by one of the players will make for a miserable day for everyone, not to mention the possibility of mistreating the course. Here is my list of the most important elements of good golf course etiquette:

Golf Above the Shoulders – Little things to enhance your game

Replace Divots

How many times have you been frustrated when you land in a hole created by a divot that was not replaced?

If only the previous person had taken the extra couple of minutes to replace their divot, this would not happen. Of course, you just kick the ball out of the hole and continue on, but technically, you are supposed to play the ball as it lies and that includes landing in a divot.

Golf Above the Shoulders – Little things to enhance your game

> It is an awful shame to see a beautiful fairway with pock marks made from divots that were not replaced. Replacing a divot is sign of a classy player.

Repair Ball Marks

As you begin to incorporate some of the ideas we are discussing in this book, you will be hitting more greens and therefore you will be making more ball marks.

Again, as with landing in a divot, how many times have you had ball marks in your line of putt, or even worse, have rolled over a ball mark only to have your putt veer off line on its' way to the hole.

If you leave a ball mark on a beautifully manicured green without fixing it, you are causing great damage to the green and ruining the putting surface. You will be guaranteed a bumpy roll that will not follow the true line.

I go nuts about this issue and I think course marshals should kick people off the course if they do not fix their ball marks.

If a ball mark is not fixed in within about one day after it is made on a hot day, the grass will begin to dry and die around the perimeter of the mark producing a permanent brown spot and depression on the green.

It only takes about 15 seconds but the impact is huge to the green and other golfers. Just insert the prongs of the tool behind the mark and push forward on the crumpled turf to move it back into the hole made by the ball. Do this at ninety degree intervals around the mark and the mark will mostly disappear. In a few days, the remainder of the mark will grow in and the putting surface will restore itself.

Do not push down on the tool and lift up the turf because that will tear the roots and the crumpled up turf will die and turn brown.

It is not the responsibility of the course maintenance crew to fix ball marks. It is the responsibility of the golfers themselves to repair their own ball marks. It is a really easy thing to do as you begin to line up your putt and walk around the green.

We all have had a ball mark or two in our line of putt and it is really annoying to have to putt over them. Fixing ball marks is also a sign of a classy player and your playing partners will be silently impressed. You will be surprised when you see them following your lead, as they also begin to fix their marks.

It is easy to fix a ball mark as shown in the next few pictures. (Note, that when these photos were taken, the green had just been spiked which allows water and oxygen to enter the green. These marks typically disappear in about three days).

With this ball mark, which is the most common, the ball crumpled up the grass at one side of the mark from the backspin. It only takes about 15 seconds to fix this mark.

Golf Above the Shoulders – Little things to enhance your game

Start by inserting the tool behind the side of the mark with the crumpled grass and push the tool toward the center of the ball mark (not shown). Next, insert the tool on one side of the mark and move that grass toward the center of the mark. This will not damage the grass.

Golf Above the Shoulders – Little things to enhance your game

Move to the other side of the mark and push the grass toward the center of the mark. The ball mark will begin to close and get smaller.

Golf Above the Shoulders – Little things to enhance your game

Continue to move around the ball mark until the hole, for the most part, disappears.

Golf Above the Shoulders – Little things to enhance your game

In this case, we entered the green about 5 times with the tool because it was a substantial ball mark on a soft green. You can see that the mark is completely closed up.

Golf Above the Shoulders – Little things to enhance your game

Finally, with your foot, or putter head, tap down the repaired area to make it smooth and puttable.

Golf Above the Shoulders – Little things to enhance your game

The ball mark is 95% gone, and in about 2 days, it will be completely restored. It only takes a few seconds to keep your golf course in top condition. Instead of playing like a "hacker", you will be a classy

player and your playing partners will begin to emulate your actions on the course as well.

Golf Above the Shoulders – Little things to enhance your game

Keep Cool

"Cool" means temper. This is a frustrating game to say the least. Nothing is more frustrating than to have a great round going only to take an 8 on the next hole! It can ruin a good score and make it hard to recover the day. But that is the nature of the game. That is what makes it so challenging. It is intriguing to our human nature like riding frightening rides at an amusing park, or putting the hottest sauce on those chicken wings. As humans, we love the excitement of the challenge and the quest to conquer that long par 5. But you must never take yourself out of the round because of a bad hole or a few bad shots. First of all, it is not fun when you lose your temper. Not fun for you and not fun for your playing partners. No one knows how to react to someone in the foursome that is cursing, yelling and slamming clubs on the ground. It puts a damper on everything. There is no place for this type of behavior on a golf course.

Golf Above the Shoulders – Little things to enhance your game

Don't walk in someone's line

> As a courtesy to the other people you are playing with, never walk in their line of putt. Leaving a scuff mark or a shoe print in someone's line is very aggravating to that person as they line up their putt. Make every effort to avoid walking in someone's line.

This also included marking your ball too. Don't mark your ball if you think the marker might be in the line. You should ask the other person if your marker will be in their line. If so, you mark the ball one putter head length to the low side of the line. The way to do this is to pick a spot in the distance that is perpendicular to the line of putt. Place your putter at a right angle to the line using the object in the distance as a reference. That way, when you place you ball back on the green, you will use the same reference point and place your ball in the opposite way to restore the proper position for your ball.

Marking a ball with the putter head

How to remove the ball from the cup

The next time you attend a pro tournament, or watch on TV, make a note of how the player or caddie removes the ball from the cup. They never walk up to the cup and bend down to pick out the ball. Instead, they stand about two feet from the cup and reach over to pick out the ball. The reason is that they do not want to put foot marks too close to the cup producing a kind of valley into the hole. They also are avoiding spike marks around the hole to spoil a good roll, and also trying not to damage the lip of the cup.

Golf Above the Shoulders – Little things to enhance your game

Rake the trap when you are done

This is self-explanatory and the reasons are obvious but it is important and worth noting. Use a rake if available. If no rake is available, then do the best you can with your club and feet. The other thing to note is to always enter the trap from the back or a point farthest from the green where it is usually a flat entry. Never enter from the green-side and have to slide down the embankment leaving deep foot prints walking over to the ball.

Broken tees

As a youngster attending Pro Tour tournaments, I noticed the caddies would pick up the pieces of the broken tees after the Pro hit his tee shot and toss them toward the tee marker. At the time it seemed like they were just trying to keep the tee box clean. Later, as the manager of a golf course it became quite apparent that there was more to cleaning up the broken tees than just keeping the tee box neat.

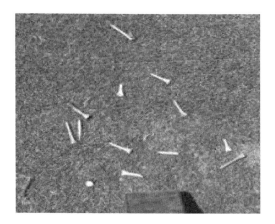

It turns out that a tee could really cause problems for the sensitive reel mowers used to cut the tee boxes. When a reel mower would hit a wooden or plastic tee, it would easily cause the cutting blades and the cutting bed to become misaligned. The results would vary from poor cutting to the mower needing expensive maintenance to realign the cutting bed.

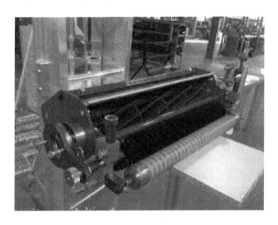

Note that the reel mowers used on a golf course sheer the grass like scissors producing a sharp cut on the top edge of each blade of grass. The rotary mower you use on your lawn rips and tears off the top of the grass leaving a jagged top edge prone to browning.

Today's equipment is not as sensitive to broken tees, however I still recommend that players pick up their broken tees and throw them over to the tee marker. It keeps the tees looking neat, and prevents the next player from having to clean up a spot from which to hit his shot.

Golf Above the Shoulders – Little things to enhance your game

Proper Dress

Golf is a game of traditions spanning XX years. It originated in Scotland, and was considered a "Gentleman's" game. Early pictures of golfers from the 19th century show them wearing suits and the women players wore special outfits and very "dressy" clothes. This trend continues through the 1930's. In the 1940's however, the dress code began to change to more casual and colorful clothes such as sported by Jimmy Demerit and others, known for their attire on the course.

Pictured here is Walter Hagan on the left and an unknown player on the right, probably sometime in the late 1930's.

The 1960's brought colors to the course and by the late 60's through today, golfers clothes are bright and, in some cases, interesting to say the least.

The point here, is that golf course attire has always been part of the game. Just as we discussed earlier that clean clubs give confidence, so does dressing nicely for a round of golf give you confidence on the course. The saying, "Dress for Success", has been around in the corporate world for a long time. It also has some relevance to golf as well. Wear nice clothes, feel good about yourself, and you just might play a little better. You will, at least, look like you know what you are doing!

Some courses have dress codes that are enforced. The illustration below shows some standards of dress for golf.

Golf Above the Shoulders – Little things to enhance your game

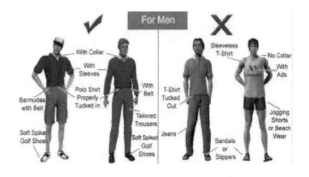

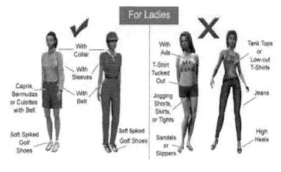

Don't take a practice divot

You see it quite often on the course. The golfer will take one or two practice swings on the fairway and take a divot each time. Many times the divot resembles a roll of sod and leaves a gaping hole in the fairway. It just isn't necessary to take a divot on a practice swing.

You should just be hitting the top of the grass or even above the grass level with a practice swing. The purpose of the practice swing is to:

- Feel the clubhead
- Establish the proper plane
- Get the right grip pressure
- Establish the rhythm of the swing
- Help eliminate some pressure and calm you down

A practice swing should not be a mini lesson on swing mechanics.

Kill Bugs, Not Grass

Biting bugs are always a nuisance on and off the course. You should always have insect repellant with you when playing a round of golf. Bug repellant can do a lot more than just keep bugs away from you, however.

Bug repellant can also damage or kill grass as shown below. This golfer was standing in the fairway when he decided to use insect repellent on his legs. The results speak for themselves as the picture shows. He left two perfect footprints where his feet protected the grass and the overspray killed the grass around his shoes!

The next time you spray insect repellent, make sure you are on a cart path.

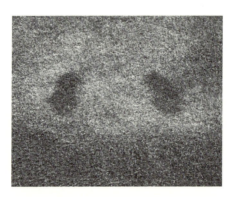

Photo curtesy of Mark Stallone, internationally known golf course architect and superintendent

Hitting Sequence Around the Green

The proper hitting sequence around the green as specified in the official USGA Rule book is that the person farthest from the hole hits first. The hitting order then follows as the group works its' way to the player closest to the hole. In other words, if someone is off the green but closer to the hole than someone who is on the green but farther away, the player farthest from the hole but on the green putts first before the person who is off the green but closer hits his chip.

I am on the fence about this one because it requires that the flag be removed for the longer putt and then put back into the hole for the closer player just off the green, and then taken out again when everyone is on the green. It could potentially slow play a little and prevent the player holding the flag from lining up his putt while waiting for the others to get on the green. Except for the pros and important amateur tournaments, golfers always start to putt when everyone is on the green. I think this works best for the average golfers. I just made note of it because of the official rule.

Line Up Your Putt in a Reasonable Time

Nothing is more distracting and annoying to a group of golfers when someone in the group (or in the group ahead), has to line up every putt like it is the 18th hole of the US Open! I think we have all played with someone like this and it is painful to watch. It is even more painful when you are standing in the fairway waiting to hit your approach shot and you are watching some guy on the green ahead lining up his putt like he is the only one on the course.

You should be lining up your putt while another player is putting and be ready when it is your time. Just make sure to keep it on the high side of the hole and concentrate on the speed. If the putt is long, your chances of making are slim, so you just want to keep it high and close enough for a tap-in or gimmie. Below is a chart of Tour averages and distances for putts:

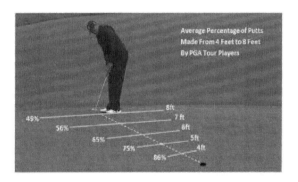

Use this chart to help you determine how to practice putting. If you can make those 8 footers and closer, you will improve you score dramatically. Just take a good guess at the longer putts, aim high and think about speed, but don't make a thesis about the line.

Keep the Pace of Play

Several points we have discussed contribute to maintaining the pace of play during a round of golf. It is important to the whole field of players that you maintain your place on the course especially on the weekends when it is very busy. Golf course starters usually allow anywhere from 8 to 10 minutes per group teeing off on the first hole. You have to try to keep your group in that same interval throughout the round. This includes minimizing the time you spend looking for lost balls and the time you require for things like the time it takes for each shot and the time it takes your group to get on and off the green. Every player will spend some time looking for a lost ball or lining up a critical putt, but you can gage your own pace of play by being aware of the distance between your group and the group in front of you. On a busy day or weekend, there should never be an open hole in front of you. The group ahead of you should still be on the green when you are on the tee box. As you know there is nothing more aggravating than slow play. We all experience it. In my younger years I actually learned how to juggle (golf balls, of course), while waiting on the tee to hit my shot. Tiger Woods can do amazing things hitting a ball up and down on a clubface. Although I don't know this as fact, but just maybe be learned how to do this while waiting to tee off.

Marking the Score Card

Always record the scores from the hole you just completed on the next tee while everyone is getting ready to hit. Never get in your cart when you have just come off the green and start asking everyone what they shot on the hole. Many times the group behind you will be waiting for you to move to the next tee so they can hit their approach shots.

Always be aware of the pace of play. Encourage your playing partners to keep things moving along.

Where to Stop Your Cart While on the Green

Always stop your cart between the green you are playing and the next tee. The point is that as soon as you exit the green, you can go right to the next tee without driving across the fairway and delaying the group behind you.

There are usually cart signs that tell you what side of the green you should be driving on. That will be the side closest to the next tee.

There is nothing more frustrating for a golfer who is waiting in the fairway to hit their approach shot up to the green when they have to wait additional time for the group on the green to exit the green on the wrong side and then drive around to the next tee.

While we are on this subject, never calculate your strokes or decide who won the hole while you are still on the green after everyone has putted out. When the last player has putted out, replace the flag and get off the green quickly so the next group can hit up.

Lost Balls

I have a "thing" about looking for lost balls. I personally use my own 5-second rule- if I can't find my ball in 5 seconds, I will drop another one. This is an extreme, for sure. A more reasonable time might be 2 or 3 minutes, but that is tops. It is horrible to play with someone that is losing their ball every other hole and spending 10 or more minutes looking for it like it was made of gold. You always find a couple of ball every time you go out anyway, so in the interest of eliminating slow play, just accept that your ball is lost and move on.

If you are consistently missing fairways and hitting your shots to where they cannot be found, then look at a couple of sections in the book on how to keep the shot in play by working with your natural shot trajectory. If you are in the trees on a regular basis, there is a systemic problem with the way you are selecting your targets, or not playing for a hook or slice.

Follow Local Cart Rules

This is probably one of the most abused areas in the game- not abiding to local daily cart rules.

Your Greens Keeper or Superintendent is trying to provide you with the best possible course conditions to make your round of golf as enjoyable as possible. A golf course takes a lot of wear and tear, especially in dry, or extremely wet conditions. When the Greens Keeper imposes the 90-degree rule, or cart path only rule, it is important to abide by the restriction so as not to damage the fairways.

Golf Above the Shoulders – Little things to enhance your game

For the novice golfer, the 90-degree rule means you drive on the cart path and then may enter the fairway at 90 degrees when you are even with your ball. After the shot, you then return to the cart path directly the way came onto the fairway and continue on the cart path.

Finally, make sure you always follow the little cart signs when they tell you to exit the fairway, usually at 50 yards and closer.

Snowman Max

In the interest of eliminating slow play, limit your score on a single hole to an 8. When you reach an eight and you are still not on the green, just pick up your ball and wait for the other players to putt out. We all have bad holes once in a while so do your fellow golfers a favor and pick up you ball and move on to the next hole.

You have to get the approval of your playing group first (best to have this discussion before you start the round), in case picking up after 8 strokes might impact any side bets or matches you have arranged.

The point here is that you want to keep a reasonable pace of play. If the rest of your group are all on the green and you are still trying to get there after 7 or 8 strokes, it might be in the interest of everyone else if you just picked up. Just remember, when your playing partners tell you to just take your time, they really don't mean it!

Play Ready Golf on Weekends

When you shoot the lowest score in your group on any one hole, you get the "honor" on the next tee by teeing off first. It is a long standing tradition in golf and means a lot to the person who has the honor on the tee.

There are times when the person with the honor is not quite ready to tee off while someone else in the group is ready to go. When the course is busy, like on the weekends, make arrangements on the first tee that you are going to play "ready golf" that day. This means that when the person with the honor is not ready to hit, the player that is ready will hit even if he/she does not have the honor. If you discuss it in advance, no one will care and your pace of play will not slow down.

Drinking on the course

There is no need for alcohol on a golf course. Many courses will allow beer, especially during golf outings, but there is no reason not to wait until the end of the round in the clubhouse for a drink or glass of beer. It does not belong on the course during play. I have seen too many incidents caused by alcohol like loud rowdy behavior. Most of the time, they are caused by people that don't belong on a golf course in the first place. Avoid going out with people that need to drink while playing.

Know the official rules

Knowing the rules of the game will speed up play and make it more enjoyable for you. Learn the rules about out-of-bounds recovery, how to deal with lateral hazards, etc.

Everyone should have a little rule book in their bag. There are smart phone apps that can put the rules at your fingertips on your cell phone.

On the back of the scorecard will be a set of local rules. These are rule modifications or variations to the standard rules for that particular golf course. Make sure you take a quick glance at the back of the card when you are playing a course for the first time.

Golf Above the Shoulders – Little things to enhance your game

EXTRA STUFF

Pin Position Indicators

Many golf courses use flag sticks that indicate the position of the cup on the green. By using a plastic ball on the flag stick, a golfer can see from down the fairway, if the cup is located in the front, middle or back of the green.

If the plastic ball, in this case a red ball, is high on the pin stick, the hole is located in the back third of the green. If the plastic ball is located low on the stick, the cup is located in the front third of the green.

Golf Above the Shoulders – Little things to enhance your game

If the plastic ball is in the middle of the stick (as in the picture above), the cup is in the middle third of the green. Make sure you check out this pin information if it is used on the course you are playing. It could mean a one or two club difference in your club selection.

Most amateur players only reach the front of the green on most approach shots and are left with a long first put which often times results in a 3-put green.

Use all of the information available to you on the course, make the right club selection, and enjoy lower scores.

Golf Above the Shoulders – Little things to enhance your game

Golf Above the Shoulders – Little things to enhance your game

How to Watch Golf

Sometimes, no matter how much you love the game, watching golf on TV can be boring. After almost 70 years of television broadcast, you still see the ball in flight after the player hits it. I have never understood why this is interesting. How does watching a little white speck against the background of the sky for 5 seconds make for interesting television viewing, and yet all the stations cover it the same way. The player hits the ball, and immediately the camera shows this little flying white spec in the sky. As viewers we have no reference as to whether the ball is going left or right or what side of the fairway it is on until it hits the ground. This is valuable broadcast time lost.

What would be much more interesting is to see how the player finishes his swing, and possibly a replay or slow motion while the ball is in flight. After the ball hits, the camera could switch to the fairway to see the roll-out.

On the positive side, the former Tour player announcers that provide insight and analysis add a great deal of value and interest to the TV coverage. Personally I think Johnny Miller is the best at this.

When the TV coverage adds visual analysis to the broadcast, you can get a lot of information and insight into swing mechanics and course management.

Even with this less than optimum TV coverage, you can still get some good information if you are looking for it.

The first thing to notice is the pre-shot routine. They all have one, and you should make note of what they are doing in the seconds before they line up and hit the ball.

Sometimes you can also notice that most players do not ground their drivers when teeing off, and note the height of the ball on the tee.

Look at the alignment and the position of their arms in relation to their body. Look at how they stand at address- you will see a lot of variation in address positions.

If you own a DVR, you can actually replay and use slow motion or stop action to see parts of the swing as shown in the pictures below. It is great to get visuals of actual real-time swings.

Use your DVR to pause and watch players in slow motion, stop action and replay.

Check out their "transition" into the downswing. I will have more to say about that later. Needless to say, the transition is key to a successful swing. This book is not about mechanics, but you need a visual of a good transition so you can work on it at the practice tee. If you have a good weight shift, the transition will just happen for you, but still check it out anyway.

When you have the opportunity to go to a Professional tournament, you have a great advantage to see all details of how the greatest players play the game.

The first thing to do is to head for the practice area. It may be difficult to see details when you are stuck in a gallery.

Golf Above the Shoulders – Little things to enhance your game

Here is the practice area for one of the Ryder Cups.

You will see many variations of practice styles. There will players who just crank out shot after shot, players with their coaches, some just taking a leisurely warm-up, while others will be seriously working on their swings. I always find this more interesting and educational than actually walking the course, or sitting behind one tee box all day. You know a picture is worth a thousand words, so here are some things to look for when you are watching the players at the practice tee:

- Address positions
- Swing plane, back and down
- Trajectory of each shot
    - High
    - Low
    - Fade
    - Draw

- The way the ball bounces
- Swing rhythm
- Shoulder Turn
- Position at the top
- Transition

The most unique warm-up session I have ever seen is that of John Daley. He starts warming up using one arm shots with his wedge or some short club. Takes a puff of a cigarette, chats a little with his entourage, and hits another one-handed shot. When I watched him, he didn't hit too many practice shots, but he looked like he was having a great time. When he finally got to the driver, it was amazing to see the distance and trajectory of the ball. He certainly generates a tremendous amount of power and speed. The trajectory starts low and rises through the flight.

I remember watching Jack Nicklaus many years ago and his shot trajectory was different. Maybe the difference was due to the equipment of the day, but Jacks' shots had a very long hang-time. The ball would rocket out into the sky and just seem to hang there for several seconds before it started back down, but you know it was traveling at the max speed of 225 feet per second all the while!

Golf Above the Shoulders – Little things to enhance your game

Join the USGA

The United States Golf Association (USGA) is the United States national association of golf courses, clubs and facilities and the governing body of golf in the U.S. and Mexico. Together with the R&A, the USGA produces and interprets the Rules of Golf. The USGA also provides a national handicap system for golfers, conducts 13 national championships, including the U.S. Open, U.S. Women's Open and U.S. Senior Open, and tests golf equipment for conformity with regulations. The USGA has provided more than $60 million in grants for underprivileged youth and individuals with disabilities. It is also the largest contributor to The First Tee program. The USGA is headquartered at Golf House in Far Hills, New Jersey.

There are various memberships available starting for as little as $10 per year. Even for that level membership you will receive a US Open cap, the official rules of golf, and a bag tag. It is a pretty good deal and you will be supporting United States golf. Go to

www.usga.org to sign up.

Golf Above the Shoulders – Little things to enhance your game

Register for a Handicap

When you join the USGA, you are able to register for a handicap through the GHIN system (Golf Handicap and Information Network). This is a service provided by the USGA for a low cost of $35 per year.

The GHIN system was created in 1981 to provide standardized handicap computations worldwide. It provides handicaps for over 2.3 million golfers.

The USGA's GHIN system is designed to allow golfers of all ability levels to complete on an equal basis. The handicap is based on a set of scores the golfer enters, and on the difficulty ratings for the courses they play.

There is a smart phone app for the GHIN system allowing you to post your scores and pick the courses you played. It is available in your app store. Just search on GHIN and you will get the result shown in the screen shot on the next page. It is a free app.

Golf Above the Shoulders – Little things to enhance your game

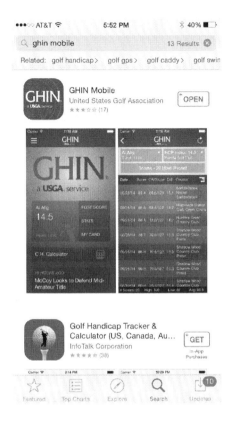

How to use the Handicap

The purpose of the handicap system is to allow players of different abilities compete against each other on a more equal basis.

When you apply a handicap to a score, the resulting modified score is call a "net" score where the score you actually shoot is call the "gross" score.

There are two ways you can use the handicap; on a hole-by-hole basis, or all at once ate the end of the round.

The first thing to do is to normalize, or equalize the handicaps for all the players. The player with the lowest handicap in the group subtracts his handicap number from the handicap numbers of the other players. Thus, the player with the lowest handicap will be giving strokes to all other players with higher handicaps. The player with the lowest handicap will never receive strokes from any other player.

Golf Above the Shoulders – Little things to enhance your game

PGA Tour Phone APP

This is an interesting and fun app available in the app store for your smart phone. It will provide real time scores for each PGA Tour stop as well as career statistics for each Tour player. Just go to your app store on your phone, search on PGA, and it will show up to be downloaded. It's totally free!

Golf Above the Shoulders – Little things to enhance your game

Little Side Games to Add to the Fun

On the internet, you can find a lot of information on different golf games to play during your round of golf. Here are a few simple challenges to add to the fun among your foursome. You keep track of each item on the scorecard and tally up the points after each round. Each point can be worth anywhere from 25 cents to $1, payable at the end of the round. Here are the items you can get points for:

- 1 point for a green in regulation
- 1 point for hitting the fairway (at least a drive of 150 yards or so)
- 2 points for a "greenie" – getting up and down from a green side sand trap
- 1 point for a par
- 3 points for a birdie

- 1 point for a 1-putt green

At the start of the round, agree on who much each point is worth. At the end of the round, add up each players' points and pay each other according to their differential. For example, if player A has 10 points, B has 8 points, C has 4 points, and D has 2 points, then player D owes C 2 points and B 6 points and A 8 points. If each point was worth 25 cents, then player D will end up paying out 16 points or $4 total. Each player does the same- paying out their point differential to each of the players above them in point totals. As you can see in this example (which is realistic), the worst case payout was only $4.

It may seem a little complicated, but it really is not and adds a little competitive excitement to the game especially if everyone is around the same skill level.

Golf Above the Shoulders – Little things to enhance your game

The Calloway Handicap System

The Calloway Handicap System was developed by Lionel Calloway (1895-1988), a Pro at Pinehurst for many years (no association with the golf company). He saw the need for a quick, one-day handicap system for golf outings and little tournaments where many of the players did not have an official golf index. In order to level the playing field, he came up with this scoring system which works well and is used in many situations. Here is a summary of how it works for your reference.

When the Callaway System is in use, all competitors tee off and play stroke play, scoring in the normal fashion with one exception - double par is the maximum score on any given hole (i.e., on a par 4, 8 is the maximum score).

Following the round, gross scores are tallied. Based on each golfer's gross score (using the double par maximum), each golfer tallies up a prescribed number of worst scores from their scorecard, then applies a second adjustment that may add or subtract additional strokes.

The result is a total that is something similar to a net score using real handicaps.

Calloway Handicap Rules:

- The higher a competitor's gross score, the more holes that player will be deducting;
- Holes deducted begin with the highest score on an individual hole.
- Scores on the 17th and 18th holes may not be deducted, or used in the handicap to eliminate cheating or purposely scoring a higher number to gain a larger handicap.
- After high scores are added together for the allowance, a second adjustment must be made; this adjustment might add or subtract 2, 1 or 0 strokes to calculate the player's final net score.
- Once the number of high scores has been calculated (from the chart), and the second adjustment is made, the player is left with a final net score.

Here is an example of how to use the system:
Let's say a player shoots a 95. Go to the chart below, and find the number 95. It says that the handicap deduction is 2 ½ worst holes. So on his scorecard, the

Golf Above the Shoulders – Little things to enhance your game

worst hole was an 8. The second worst hole was a 7 and the third worst hole was also a 7. We need add up the two worst holes and half of the third worst. We will have a 15 for the two worst holes, and a 3 ½ for half of the third worst hole. When half scores are calculated, always round up, so we will have a 4 for the half hole. The total deduction is 19 strokes. There is one more score adjustment to be made. Find the "95" score again and go down to the bottom line. There you will find a +2 for the adjustment. You add this +2 to the 19 strokes and get a total handicap of 21 to be subtracted from the gross score of 95, giving a 74 for the net score.

As a reference, you can print out the chart on the next page, fold it up and stick it in the rulebook you keep in your golf bag.

Just remember, you cannot use the 17th and 18th holes in your calculations for the worst holes to deduct.

The Calloway Handicap System

Gross (using double par max.)					Handicap Deduction
		70	71	72	Scratch
73	74	75			1/2 of Worst Hole

Copyright 2017 All Rights Reserved

Golf Above the Shoulders – Little things to enhance your game

76	77	78	79	80	Worst Hole
81	82	83	84	85	1 1/2 Worst Holes
86	87	88	89	90	2 Worst Holes
91	92	93	94	95	2 1/2 Worst Holes
96	97	98	99	100	3 Worst Holes
101	102	103	104	105	3 1/2 Worst Holes
106	107	108	109	110	4 Worst Holes
111	112	113	114	115	4 1/2 Worst Holes
116	117	118	119	120	5 Worst Holes
121	122	123	124	125	5 1/2 Worst Holes
126	127	128	129	130	6 Worst Holes
-2	-1	0	+1	+2	**Handicap Adjustment**

Golf Above the Shoulders – Little things to enhance your game

The Scramble Format

This is a format of play that does not incorporate handicaps. You can use twosomes, threesomes, or foursomes for the individual teams, and one sore will be recorded for each team. Larger teams will result in lower scores.

Everyone on the team will hit a tee shot on each hole. The team will then, decide which of the tee shots is best for the hole. All team members will agree on the best tee shot to use and pick up all of the other balls that will not be used. The second shot for each player will be hit from the spot of the tee shot that is being used. Each player will place his ball within a club-head length of the original shot, but you do not have to put your ball in a previous divot. All following shots are played this way including putts on the green until the ball is in the hole.

Some Scramble formats require each player to use a minimum number of tee shots to prevent a player who may be an excellent driver off the tee, from using all of his/her tee shots. The rules could specify that each player in the group use at least four tee shots. This requires a little strategy in choosing which tee shot to use. On shorter holes you may want to use the tee shot from a short hitter in order to use up one of the minimums.

If you are able to assemble a team of players with different strengths, your team will be able to shoot a does not result in individual scores, only one team score.

Golf Above the Shoulders – Little things to enhance your game

The Better Ball of Partners

This playing format is exactly what it sounds like. Teams can be 2, 3, or 4 players and everyone plays their own ball. After each hole, the best score is recorded for the team. At the end of the round, players will have an individual score, and a Better Ball Score for the team.

The Better Ball score may be a net score, or a gross score. This means that if handicapped scores are used, then the final team score will be a net score. If no handicaps are used, the final team score will be a gross score.

Alternate Shot

The Alternate Shots format is a good format for mixed couples, meaning male-female teams. Just as in a scramble format, only one score is recorded for the team. There are two ways to play this format; in the first case, the same player hits the tee shot on each hole, then the second player hits the second shot, etc. until the hole is completed and the ball is in the hole. In this version, the player hitting the tee shot is determined before the first hole begins and must continue to hit all tee shots on the rest of the holes.

In the second version, each shot is hit by alternating players and the alternate play continues onto the next tee. So, on a par 5 for example, if player A hits the tee shot, player B hits the second, and player A hits the third onto the green. Player B will hit the first putt, player A hits the second putt and makes par, that hole is over and player B will now hit the tee shot on the next hole. This is a true alternate shot sequence. Personally, I prefer this form of Alternate Shot because it levels the field so that all teams compete on a more equal basis.

Epilogue

I hope you have learned something new from this little book. Golf is the game of a lifetime for men, women and children. It is a great way to stay connected to friends and loved ones for many years.

Golf builds character, patience and relationships.

Made in the USA
Middletown, DE
27 July 2022